DATE DUE

AP2 4'00			
OO.9 T⅄W			
⅄V 1 6'00			
NO 6'00			
DE2 0'00			

DEMCO 38-296

KAIZEN
STRATEGIES
—— FOR ——
SUCCESSFUL
LEADERSHIP

改善

KAI   ZEN

change   +   good

=

improvement

KAIZEN
STRATEGIES
— FOR —
SUCCESSFUL
LEADERSHIP

How to take your
organization into the future

TONY BARNES

PITMAN PUBLISHING
128 Long Acre, London WC2E 9AN

A Division of Pearson Professional Limited

First published in Great Britain 1996

© Pearson Professional Limited 1996

British Library Cataloguing in Publication Data
A CIP catalogue record for this book can be obtained
from the British Library.

ISBN 0 273 61709 5

3 5 7 9 10 8 6 4

Typeset by Northern Phototypesetting Co. Ltd, Bolton
Printed and bound in Great Britain by
Biddles Ltd, Guildford and King's Lynn

*The Publishers' policy is to use paper manufactured
from sustainable forests.*

THE EUROPE JAPAN CENTRE

The Europe Japan Centre is part of a major Japanese corporation, the Osaka Gas Group, with offices in Japan, the USA, Singapore and the UK. The Centre uses these international links to help its clients succeed on a global platform by offering them high quality research and human resources and management development expertise. Drawing on the staff's extensive personal experience of business practices around the world, the Centre offers a unique blend of *the Best of East and West.*

THE BEST OF EAST AND WEST

The aim of the Europe Japan Centre is to be a major international influence in business.

To achieve this, we must be flexible, pro-active, informed and adaptable, and our core businesses of research, education and development should be delivered to our clients in a unique way by combining the best of East and West.

Our goal is always to be one step ahead, to anticipate the needs of our clients and to fulfil those needs to the very best of our ability.

We are committed to continuously improving everything we do, by developing our people and working together as a team.

CONTENTS

PREFACE TO THE SERIES

'Kaizen' offers something new to all organizations and to the people in and around those organizations: a philosophy and framework that encourages them to continuously set higher standards of performance and to achieve new goals in terms of customer satisfaction, sales and, ultimately, profit.

Kaizen is not a new concept. Literally, it simply means improvement, and many people when they hear it explained for the first time look relieved and say they have been doing it for years without knowing what it was called. This is not surprising; most people in the West, as well as in the East, have a desire to improve their work, their relationships, their lives, and many try hard to do so. But, in a management sense, improvement and Kaizen are not synonymous: Kaizen offers far more.

It is the intention of this series to explore exactly how Kaizen can offer more to organizations in the West, how it can help them pull step-by-step ahead of their competitors. In doing this, the Europe Japan Centre has unashamedly extended and modified the original Japanese concept of Kaizen, and has sought to combine the strengths of Western organizations with those of Japan. We are talking about Kaizen for the West, not about a slavish imitation of a concept 'not invented here'.

It seems to us that the time is right for this approach. In the increasingly competitive global market, companies are looking for ideas and practices that work, wherever they originate, not so that they can do exactly the same themselves, but so that they can adapt them to suit their own culture. At the same time, the recession in Japan and the questioning of many practices to which Japan's success has been attributed, means that Japan too is looking for new management ideas, and that for the West now to follow Japanese practices without adaptation would make no sense. Underlying the whole series, therefore, is our theme of 'the Best of East and West'.

Our approach to Kaizen focuses very clearly on the people element; each title is devoted to a group of people who are key to the success of an organization: leaders of the organization (*Kaizen Strategies for Successful Leadership*), the whole workforce (*Kaizen Strategies for Winning Through People*) and customers, be they internal or external (*Kaizen Strategies for Customer Care*).

For people who have looked on Kaizen principally as a set of processes for improving manufacturing, this approach may seem unusual. It is the experience of the Europe Japan Centre, however, that the most vital determinant in achieving lasting and continuous improvement is the attitude and behaviour of people, and that Kaizen strategies cannot work without the commitment of the people putting them into practice. Although most organizations may know this theoretically, their human resources practices, their leadership styles and their attitudes to customers by no means always reflect this knowledge. This series aims to help bridge this gap between theory and practice.

Researchers at the Europe Japan Centre draw on a worldwide network of contacts to locate and analyze the latest human resources and management ideas and trends. Our consultants and trainers combine these new thoughts with the Centre's practical experience in working with companies in the UK and continental Europe, so that our own services too are continuously improved. The awareness sessions, seminars, workshops and consultancy we offer are designed to help organizations of all sizes and types build on their strengths and create new, more effective strategies through their people. This series of books outlines some of our experiences, and brings together examples of the different approaches of organizations around the world.

The focus of the Europe Japan Centre and of these books is not, however, past practice or even current practice. What we are seeking to do is to stimulate thought, to concentrate the thinking of organizations on the future. Kaizen through people is one way of bringing the future closer, of inventing the future you want for your organization. We hope this series will help you do this in your own way, and we hope too that you will let us know of your success.

Chris Patrick
Director, Europe Japan Centre
September 1995

FOREWORD

This is a book based partly on 'Kaizen', a powerful Japanese business philosophy whose value as the driving cultural force behind many large and small organizations in every business sector in the West has already been unquestionably proven.

The book is also based on that perennial issue *leadership*, whose styles, characteristics and practices have been examined and discussed in the minutest detail in tens of hundreds of books and articles.

However, there has not been a book that explains exclusively and completely the Kaizen approach to leadership and the very particular role and responsibilities of leaders in the open and participatory environments of Kaizen-driven businesses.

This book aspires to fill that gap. It sets out to inform and advise you about much that I have called 'tomorrow's' businesses and 'tomorrow's' leaders – although, in truth, many such businesses are already operating highly successfully. They have adopted Kaizen and adapted it to suit Western social, organizational and interpersonal cultures to create continuous improvement (or learning) organizations, and leaders whose great *personal* power and influence is exercised in such a way that harmony, participatory sharing, consensus, team structure, free-flowing communication and employee empowerment sits confidently and comfortably with the achievement of market share, net profit, return on assets, earnings per share and corporate success. I call this creating a marriage between the best from the East and the best from the West.

I believe strongly that learning from how organizations such as Unipart, Rolls Royce, General Motors, European Components and Nissan (UK) have reformed their structures, styles, systems and the roles of their leaders can help every business succeed more effectively.

This book will help you understand Kaizen and leadership. Sir Peter Parker in his book *For Starters** wrote:

> 'A manager's success in fusing all three dimensions (economic, entrepreneurial and social) depends on his or her capacity to lead. People prefer being led to being managed. I suppose that is because the process of good leadership makes a leader understand how much depends on others. He has to listen to them, and that means being accessible.'

In the final chapter Sir Peter wrote these succinct but very telling words which, for me, describe how close yet how far apart leadership in Eastern and Western business is:

> 'Takeo Fujisawa, co-founder of Honda, was asked to compare Japanese and Western management. He was as polite as he could be: it was 95 per cent the same, and different in all important respects. Five per cent may be a tiny figure, but revolutions are led by minorities. (The) combined economic and social attitude, both in the management of their economy and in the management of their enterprise, is what lies behind the record of Japan's post-war resurgence.'

Tony Barnes

---

*Jonathan Cape, 1989

ACKNOWLEDGEMENTS

I wish to thank the many hundreds of delegates who have attended the in-house and public seminars at which I have spoken on Kaizen and leadership: their enthusiasm and searching questions have been key reasons for writing this book.

Similarly, my colleagues at the Europe Japan Centre have not only repeatedly asked me to put down on paper my thoughts and experiences of working with companies that have embarked on the journey towards adopting *Westernized* Kaizen, but also supported me throughout the book's preparation.

The administrative staff at EJC and Pitman Publishing (researchers, typists, reviewers and editors) have been wonderful; the book is as much a product of their personal and collective contributions and effort as it is of mine. My thanks too go to my wife, Marilyn, for all her support and encouragement.

Finally, I must thank Marek Gitlin for all that he did to make this book a reality.

INTRODUCTION

Ask a cross-section of the public in the West to describe their visualization of a Japanese leader and invariably you will hear about *stereotypes* – of military leaders (from either the Second World War or the classic periods of Samurai domination in the 14th and 15th Centuries), emperors, business autocrats and bureaucrats, and politicians. Occasionally, you will hear a specific name from Japan's pantheon of leading physicists, fashion designers, artists (painters, sculptors, potters), playwrights, actors and movie directors, restaurateurs, authors and sportsmen.

The range of responses tends to be limited, however, not because Japan has never produced world-class leaders, but because we generally get to know very little about them; we know far more about European and American leaders than we do about Japan's. On the face of it this is quite natural, yet it belies how much we have been and continue to be influenced by leaders who, in the context of this book, have shaped our leisure, consumer, industrial and financial lives. None of the responses to my question, then, are wholly incorrect but, by the same token, few are wholly accurate and give a complete picture.

Ask the same question of people in Japan and, quite expectedly, the answers will be more precise than general. In recent years and as a consequence of post-war management theory particularly, the ideal of a Japanese leader has come to be seen as a man who has worked his way up in a company, is disciplined, loyal and self-effacing, who inspires by his actions rather than his words, and who listens, guides, offers counsel and is of his people rather than being a dictator who keeps himself apart from those whom he deems to rule. It is clear from this description that many Japanese people in some ways *still* greatly admire, and emulate, the qualities – sometimes the fairytale qualities – of the great Samurai: a fearless fighter but capable of being moved to tears by beauty; noble but ruthless; unforgiving but open to novel ideas from any common foot soldier; courteous but dismissive; a true leader but prepared to let others dominate at strategy meetings. In other words, the very stuff of legend that compares with our own tastes of Arthurian chivalry. The Samurais' code of conduct, (*Bushido*), is still often referred to in Japan. For example, the 'Three Heroes' of Japan's unification in the 16th- and early-17th Centuries are still quoted in boardrooms. These heroes are Toyotomi Hideyoshi who rose from humble beginnings to rule over the whole of Japan. He is used now as a symbol of Japan's *nouveaux riches*. Oda Nobunaga, supposedly a man of quick decision and foresight, died before he could realize his dream of ruling Japan. He is used now as a symbol of tragic genius. Tokugawa Ieyasu, founder of the Tokugawa Shogunate, is remembered as a man of patience and great strength in administration and organization. He is used now as a symbol of Japan's élite bureaucracy. The qualities of the Three Heroes do not describe the whole picture, however. The Westernizing of many Japanese businesses since 1945 has introduced new attitudes and styles into business leadership that have tempered the earlier fiery and mercurial styles of leadership. Today's best known leaders are people like Akio Morita, co-founder of the Sony Corporation; and Yasuhiro Nakasone, Prime Minister from 1982–87.

In Japan today, business leaders of every hue exist. There are still those who consider themselves Shoguns and run their companies like personal fiefdoms with all the attendant implications for 'indentured' employees; but on the other hand there are leaders who revere the teachings of Drs W. Edwards Deming and J. M. Juran and, consequently, consider employees, customers, communication, training, sharing, empowerment and quality integral and inseparable components of the organizational leadership complex.

I refer in this book to their companies as Kaizen companies, to differentiate their employee practices, style of leadership, organizational structure and internal company processes from traditional – or non-Kaizen – Western and Japanese companies.

These companies are not only the large global conglomerates whose product brands are household names (Matsushita, Sony, Komatsu, Canon, Fuji, Nissan, Toyota, Kawasaki, etc). Many are small, family-run concerns serving a local population but whose success – and importantly, the *basis* of that success – has brought them to national (sometimes international) attention.

It is the spirit of leadership in these companies, large and small, representing every market sector from food to shipbuilding, that I shall examine in this book, and whose style of leadership – in support of a Kaizen approach – I shall present as having important elements of an effective way in which tomorrow's business will be run. These leaders are individually as different from the negative stereotypes of Japanese business leaders as Charles Handy, one of Britain's foremost management and organizational theorists and practitioners, is from the Union Jacked and phlegmatic John Bull.

I intend this book to be an easy book to read: I have adopted a narrative style (as I do in my seminars) and divided the book into just five simple chapters whose key lessons are immediately accessible. In brief, the chapters cover the following principal themes:

Chapter 1

This chapter will outline the current changes taking place in businesses in the West and the way they are likely to develop over the next decade, focusing particularly on the aspects which affect the role of leaders; that is to say, as a result of technological change, new patterns of competition and new research into human behaviour, many businesses in the West are, in the late 20th Century, characterized by a shift away from centralized corporate policies and financial controls. The new organizations tend to rely on:

- teams, rather than individuals
- networks, rather than hierarchical structures
- highly-trained employees, rather than capital
- the Kaizen approach, encouraging flexibility and continuous improvement.

The chapter will also include a brief introduction to the principles of Kaizen, which I will build on in later chapters in relation to leadership. Case studies will be provided to show examples of successful changes in company organization, and the reasons for and implications of the changes.

Chapter 2

In this chapter I will examine first, the most important characteristics that leaders will increasingly need in the new business environment, and second, how leaders will need to spend their time. It will develop the idea of the leader as a 'coach' or 'educator'.

Characteristics will include the ability to 'let go', to listen as well as to speak, the demonstration of respect for others, to help nurture creativity and vision, to establish a no-blame culture.

Leaders will need to spend their time understanding global trends, promoting the company's mission and vision, motivating and developing people, allowing change to occur, and making alliances. Case studies from Japan will highlight in particular the strength and success of Japanese leaders in building global networks.

In addition, case studies will be used to support these topics.

Chapter 3

This chapter will deal with the question of devolving responsibility throughout organizations, so improvement can occur naturally and continuously in all parts of the company.

More specifically, it will cover:

- how to 'let go' and what to delegate
- how to empower and support people successfully
- how to help other people in the organization become 'leaders' within their teams, groups and the organization as a whole
- 'leaderless' organizations: focusing on companies such as Dettmers Industries (winner of the 1993 US award for one of the best small companies to work for in America), which are moving towards rotating team leaders and leaderless units.

Chapter 4

In the light of the changes described in the previous chapter, this one will examine the role of strategic planning in the organizations of tomorrow and explore the role of leaders and other people in the organization throughout the planning process.

Specific issues to be covered include:

- using a Kaizen approach to planning
- linking the company's vision and mission to strategic planning
- cross-company and interdepartmental involvement in planning
- how leaders can encourage successful planning.

Examples showing the best of Eastern and Western management and new styles of international practice will be used.

Chapter 5

In this final chapter I will outline a programme to help Western businesses develop an organizational culture and operating processes based on the best from the East and the best from the West.

1

WHAT WILL TOMORROW'S ORGANIZATIONS LOOK LIKE?

改善

INTRODUCTION

There have been many changes of emphasis in Western businesses during the past quarter century. The development of satellite companies; zero-based budgeting; growth through acquisition and diversification; portfolio management; divestment and consequent focus on core competencies; globalization; Management by Objectives; intrapreneuring; down-sizing (or right-sizing); risk management; customer care; IT-based systems management; organizational flattening; One-Minute Managing; Total Quality Management; BPR – have each in their time influenced the shape and culture of companies. But the biggest and what I am convinced will be the most influential paradigm change has yet to be widely felt.

The direct beneficiaries of this movement, more so even than customers, will be employees. People are often surprised when I say that employees are the most important people for any business, as it has become a cliché to say customers are the most important. But without good employees, there can be no customers. The movement toward employees can be described crudely as humanistic or, to use current jargon, holistic. Employees are once again being acknowledged as the most powerful determinator of corporate success; only

改

this time, having been starved of investment for the better part of the last decade, they are at the centre of vigorous attention focusing on the culture and environment in which they work, and the leadership and management processes to which they respond.

The change from romancing product and technology *per se* to emphasizing the quality and skills of the employees who drive these non-human resources will involve considerably more than reinvesting in training and development, though breathing new life into this sometimes moribund function is an absolute prerequisite if companies are to take full advantage of their post-recession survival. The change will be revolutionary and require of business leaders a marked shift in focus from systems to processes and from the inanimate organizational structures to the animate, that is to the workforce. Spinning out from this will be the creation of teams as the defining and fundamental unit within workforces, encouragement of cross-functional collaboration, more open communication internally and externally, the collapse of traditional pyramid hierarchies, the demise of conventional power bases and the consequent sharing of decision-making by those closest to the point of action, and the implementation of new management processes, behaviours and thinking.

This wholesale change will result in manufacturing and administration technologies being seen as nothing more remarkable than the contemporary *tools* of today's employees, rather than as their "newsworthy" masters. And outputs, whether these are products, cost savings, customer services, reduced wastage, increased market share, higher quality, greater choice, cycle-time reduction or net profit, will be the consequence of highly-trained and educated employees using those tools and management processes opportunistically to best advantage. In other words, the shift in emphasis will be away from new machinery and to the people who operate it. In totality, the emphasis will be on *organizational integration*, reaching the point where everything – plant, performance systems, values, vision, competencies, management, training, culture, corporate goals – is aligned. And the factor that will hold all this together is leadership.

Leadership does not happen of itself, and certainly *not* as the consequence of a person being given authority or acquiring power. There are distinct leadership competencies that can be learnt, as can the ability to exercise leadership responsibilities. It is not only those at the top of an organization who need leadership skills (and, incidentally, frequently need coaching in *people* leadership skills as distinct from corporate leadership skills): the same skills must be syndicated down through the entire organization to team level, where corporate alignment, interaction and the commitment to achieve goals will thrive or fail.

Some of what I am saying here is derived from the work of Professor George Labovitz of the Boston School of Management. In an interview published in the May/June 1995 edition of *European Quality** he used a fascinating metaphor to describe the link that exists between such fundamental employee units as teams (and the individuals in them) and their company. He used the metaphor to describe his concept of integration. (In Kaizen companies the word used would be 'harmony'.)

---

*Volume 2, Number 3

改

Labovitz said,

> 'Fractals are a surprisingly good metaphor for what we mean by integrated culture. Fractals are self-replicating parts that reflect the whole, as the leaf of a fern is a replica of the whole.'

I believe his metaphor is understandable; what he is saying is, teams – in all their activities, behaviours, attitudes and goals – must reflect in microcosm those of the organization of which they are the basic constituent. He further implies that teams are not merely the smallest denominator of organizational structure, ie the tip of a leaf, they *are* the leaves (where a leaf is a metaphor for a department or division) that exist for and because of the organization via mutually supportive life processes. In other words, an organization is its people: they – teams and individuals – gain their identity, culture, values and *raison d'être* from the organization, and the organization gains its life (growth and marketplace domination) from the replicated successes of its employees. For this, teams must be integrated into the whole; and as I said, leadership is the prime factor that will keep any plant facing into the sun.

Clearly, though, leadership itself must be sustained by some powerful force if it is to fulfil its own *raison d'être*. And so it is in Kaizen companies, where this organizational philosophy is wholly pervasive and compelling.

KAIZEN

You might not have heard of Kaizen, but you will have heard of – and perhaps be personally familiar with the activities related to – Total Quality Management (TQM). Think of TQM and you will begin to understand Kaizen, for much that we in the West know of as TQM stems from Kaizen.

Kaizen (the word combines the Japanese characters *Kai*, which means 'change', and *Zen*, which means 'good') translates as 'improvement.' In the West it is commonly taken to mean, as a management concept, 'continuous improvement'.

It is a Japanese concept, a philosophy, though it is highly amenable to Westernization thereby creating a very influential culture which blends the primacy and benefits of teamwork from Kaizen with the West's strength of individuality.

According to Kaizen, progress is achieved less through momentous single leaps forward than via unceasing small changes to the hundreds of thousands of details associated with producing products or services, originating from the idea downstream to the point of sale and after-sales service. The premise on which change is based is that in Kaizen there is no such thing as perfection; that is to say, no progress, product, relationship, system or structure ever achieves the ideal where it cannot be improved by yet further reducing waste, shaving off more cost, getting more value from existing investment in plant or raw materials, taking less time, improving service, increasing reliability or, in terms of leadership, strengthening team cohesion, enhancing motivation or reinforcing competencies. In a nutshell, nothing stands still in a Kaizen company; there is no *status quo*. In a sense, what Kaizen aims to serve, the perfect product, is never attainable: there is always another day or another person to find an improvement.

For this reason, outputs are referred to as 'quotas' or 'standards' rather than 'targets': according to Dr W. Edwards

改

Deming, the American originator of some Kaizen processes, once a 'target' has been met there can be a tendency to slacken-off effort; a 'standard', on the other hand, promotes effort to beat it, thereby establishing a new standard and a new threshold.

Through adhering to the view that every aspect of a production cycle is always open to scrutiny and improvement, and through always seeing quality as the ultimate goal, Japan's manufacturing expertise and prowess has inexorably grown and rolled over the world during the 50 years since the end of the Second World War. Millions upon millions of tiny improvements have produced a veritable litany of evolutionary advances which, collectively, have taken Japan from a 'nowhere' nation to the forefront of global trading. How this has changed Japan is evident for everyone to see; in purely financial terms, for example, Japanese consumers are the richest in the world. The total amount on deposit in Japan's post office savings system exceeds $2 trillion – more than double Italy's GDP.

South Korean industries are taking the same approach: Kaizen, adapted to suit their culture and business infrastructure (which is very different from Japan's), is the philosophical driver behind their unremitting climb to the top.

The question is, can Kaizen work in a Western business? The answer is unequivocally yes, but of course it is not simply a case of 'bolting on' Kaizen as a quick-fix panacea for corporate ills.

Kaizen is a philosophy, an attitude, a way of thinking and behaving. It is primarily a cultural force; secondarily it is a set of compelling processes such as the PDCA Cycle, Kaizen Circles, Statistical Process Control, Visible Management and

Cross-functional Collaboration (*see* the panel on pages 15–20 for an explanation of these processes). These are what I call Kaizen's instruments; its *principles* – the actions that make the philosophy tangible – are these:

KAIZEN'S PRINCIPLES

I consider Kaizen to have *ten* principles:

1 Focus on customers

Kaizen's *primary* focus is product quality, but the ultimate purpose is higher customer satisfaction; therefore, the final beneficiaries of Kaizen's instruments and its principles are customers. Anything which does not add value to a product or enhance customer delight should be eliminated, according to Kaizen; activities which do not serve Kaizen's primary focus are, by definition, an irredeemable cost and thus a burden which cannot be justified.

2 Make improvements continuously

It is within our nature when we have accomplished a task successfully to turn our attention to something new. In Kaizen companies an accomplishment is not the end of the matter but merely the completion of one step before the next. There is no end, for today's standards, designs, costs, and so on will not meet tomorrow's demands, and Kaizen employees know that it is far more cost- and time-effective to improve an existing product than start each time from a blank sheet of paper. Hence, improvements are planned and executed

改

ceaselessly. An upshot of this is, for example, the stream of 'new' electronic consumer goods which reach the world's domestic markets with bewildering speed and regularity from Japanese factories. In truth, few of these products are really new; the great majority are previous products improved to satisfy today's tastes and budgets. But it works: *we* are seduced by the choice and by the extent to which our wants are constantly fulfilled, and the *manufacturers* enjoy new marketing opportunities each time. The costs to them of constantly improving today's products are consequently relatively minimal and, because of that, the range offered at any one time coupled with the knowledge that new products are always coming on-stream, means they can afford to drop or change an improvement that does not work.

Occasionally, the process of constantly and painstakingly reviewing and improving a product produces an absolute world-class innovation: Sony's Walkman is the outcome of Akio Morita asking the simple question, How much larger than a cassette does a cassette player really have to be? And using *existing* technology and components reconfigured to suit the objective he gave us the answer. He could then have turned his attention to something new. But he improved the original Walkman, and within six months a better model was on the market. He then set up a team to apply the same development processes to the miniaturization of televisions.

Such companies as Sony know that total quality is the *sine qua non* of survival.

3 Acknowledge problems openly

By fostering a no-blame culture, employees in Kaizen companies feel able to admit errors, point out process weaknesses and ask for help. Such openness is considered a strength for it enables problems to be contained and resolved very rapidly, and for opportunities to be realized equally quickly. In closed organizations, problems are either not admitted or kept hidden; they then tend to be handled conspiratorially or by only an intimate coterie of staff where silence might well be guaranteed, but by whose isolation, ideas may be equally closed and limited.

4 Promote openness

Compartmentalization, territoriality, proprietoriality and ringfencing are typical within very traditional non-Kaizen businesses. None of this engenders the sharing, cross-functionality, openness and leadership visibility typical of Kaizen organizations. Knowledge is personal power in the former companies; in the latter shared knowledge, and the communication channels which support it, are the source of greater corporate efficiency.

5 Create work teams

Teams are the building blocks of corporate structure within Kaizen organizations. Individual employees give the team to which each belongs a reputation for efficiency, performance, and improvement; the team gives its members rank, status and identity; and in a two-way exchange of recognition teams and their leaders serve each other to achieve personal success, and reward. Through its employees belonging to various overlapping teams (a work team, a year team (composed of employees who joined their company at the same time),

改

Kaizen Circles (the successor to Quality Circles) and cross-functional project teams), the company gains advantage from its employees *networking*. This draws employees into corporate life and reinforces mutual ownership, collective responsibility and company-centredness. It also strengthens openness, sharing and communication.

Two by-products of this are first, discipline is maintained by peer pressure (and leadership) to ensure that no single person is allowed to upset intra-team balance and inter-team harmony and second, everyone is encouraged to take advantage of education and training to ensure that personal contributions add value to their team's outputs.

6 Manage projects through cross-functional teams

It is a requirement in Kaizen and Kaizen-influenced organizations that projects are planned and executed using cross-departmental and cross-functional resources, even resources from outside the company. The Boeing Aircraft Corporation, for example, used internal cross-functional teams in conjunction with future customer and supplier teams when designing and commissioning production of its new aeroplane, the Boeing 777. This approach to product design and development and project implementation was directly influenced by the Kawasaki-led consortium which worked with Boeing to manufacture fuselage and wing sections. The benefits of cross-functionalism (sometimes known as 'simultaneous engineering') were tangible to Boeing: not only were production cycles and costs reduced significantly (compared to those associated with its other great aeroplane, the 747), but waste (wasted materials, time and effort) was controlled to the *n*th degree and, ultimately and critically importantly, the company's customers got precisely what they needed to satisfy their own customers. (I was touched to learn that Boeing had fitted gas-operated struts to its lavatory seats, so that they closed quietly, in response to British Airways' observation that English passengers were embarrassed when the seats slammed down audibly!)

7 Nurture the right relationship processes

The Japanese dislike adversarial and confrontational relationships (those that can accompany purely results-driven and blame cultures), and do all they can to ensure that harmony is maintained by investing much in interpersonal skills training for all staff, but especially for managers and team leaders whose responsibility it is to ensure that relationship processes and protocols are the very best. Western supervisors who have joined Kaizen companies have been surprised by the huge amount of time spent on relationship skills education for team leaders, but by ensuring that the processes are sound and relationships are designed to nurture employee fulfilment the company's investment is repaid through employee commitment and loyalty.

8 Develop self-discipline

Self-discipline at work comes naturally to many Japanese people who, through schooling, religion and social norms, find conforming to the natural order both comforting and an affirmation of inner strength and wholeness. This can nonetheless demand self-sacrifice in the sense that harmonizing with one's team colleagues and the company credo can

改

mean keeping one's essential individuality in check, and being prepared to put company, team and team leader before one's self and family. (Some Japanese businessmen reassert their individuality at karaoke bars and by joining any number of hobby and fantasy clubs which allow them to escape from the conformity and uniformity of working life; I understand that the Harley-Davidson and American Police Patrol clubs are the most popular in Tokyo.)

To a Westerner, this is the most difficult of Kaizen's principles to accept: conformity, consensus and loss of individuality sit less comfortably with us – it is the principle that, therefore, requires the most adaptation and management.

9 Inform every employee

Sharing information is vitally important in Kaizen companies. Team leaders and managers acknowledge that employees cannot be expected to participate beyond their everyday tasks – in, for example, their company's suggestion system, Kaizen (or Quality) Circles, project teams – if they are kept in the dark concerning company mission, values, products, performance, people and plans. Keeping everyone informed makes corporate challenges *personal* challenges. It is also an essential step in creating a knowledge-based culture.

10 Enable every employee

Through multiskill training, encouragement, decision-making responsibility, access to data sources and budgets, feedback, job-rotation and reward Kaizen employees are empowered to materially influence their own and their company's affairs. Sharing power in this way and devolving it to those at the point of action takes managerial courage, but in Kaizen companies managers and team leaders who demonstrate confidence in themselves and their people by delegating responsibilities are more powerful than those who feel scared to let go. It is important to recognize the view in Kaizen that an organization's capacity to enhance existing skills and learn new ones is a powerful competitive advantage.

These, then, are Kaizen's principles. Their obvious simplicity and commonsensical nature surprises many business leaders with whom I discuss them; they are equally surprised when I caution them not to run away with the idea that their simplicity means a single and quick introduction, especially if the existing framework is traditionally Western. I also emphasize that while the management of a Kaizen programme must be led and controlled overtly from the top, the challenges on lower-level team leaders to change the attitudes, thinking and behaviour of employees should never be underestimated. For this reason, team leaders must be selected and educated most carefully – a point I amplify under the heading further on in 'Kaizen leadership skills'.

KAIZEN'S INSTRUMENTS

Kaizen has gathered a number of techniques and tools under its wing, some like Quality Circles and Just-in-Time inventory control, have been developed from Deming's and Juran's initial thoughts and 're-exported' to the West as stand-alone processes; others, such as Visible Management (or Leadership) and

▶

改

Process Oriented Management have grown from within Japanese practices and are integral components of the 'Kaizen way'.

You might be familiar with a number of the following instruments, as many have been adopted in the West as processes within TQM. Taken as a whole, the list of instruments describes how Kaizen is made tangible as part of everyday tasks, particularly in production environments.

Suggestion Systems

The difference between a non-Kaizen suggestion *scheme* and a Kaizen suggestion *system* is found in the subtle but telling difference between the two italicized words. A Kaizen suggestion system is wholly inclusive, driven by consensus, activated by teams, supervised by team leaders, and an important benchmark of team and team leader performance. It is a process, in other words, owned by employees though designed to benefit their company. It features strongly in in-company communication as both a trigger for and a focus of personal contribution and team loyalty.

Suggestions are frequently the subject of Kaizen (or Quality) Circle meetings, and can encompass any idea, large or small, novel or mundane, concerning any aspect of company life, from training programmes to reducing environmental pollution. Employees in a typical large Kaizen company will each contribute between 30 and 60 suggestions per year, though it is not remarkable that the most observant and creative employees can contribute upwards of 1,000 suggestions each per year. Clearly, the majority of these will have negligible value, but if such ideas nevertheless represent even tiny improvements they will likely be adopted; and as I have said, one small improvement might not represent measurable progress but thousands over a period can propel huge advances.

Quality (Control) Circles

These were originally *ad hoc* groups of volunteers, led by a senior shopfloor worker, who met to discuss and resolve local quality problems as part of Japan's country-wide strategy for national recovery after the Second World War. By 1972 recovery was substantially underway and Quality Circles developed into Kaizen Circles, still voluntary but with the much wider remit of finding process improvements; and this is the function of QCs (or KCs) in Japan today: the term *quality* is a carry-over from the 1960s and no longer fully describes the horizon over which these groups cast their attention.

Process Oriented Management

Whilst Kaizen companies are as driven by the need for positive outcomes as their non-Kaizen counterparts, the emphasis in Kaizen is on the process – or the 'how' – of achieving the required results. But POM goes further than merely designing effective processes; Kaizen team leaders need to know *why* a process works, whether it can be modified or replicated for elsewhere in the company and how it can be improved. These are the sorts of issues that might well be the subject of suggestion system ideas and Kaizen Circle meetings.

Visible Management (or Visible Leadership)

We might refer to this as Management By Walking Around, (MBWA) though in Kaizen companies VM (or VL) goes beyond a team leader or a manager appearing on the shopfloor now and then to be amongst the people. Visible Management is an inextricable component of a Kaizen team leader's role; it requires of him or her exactly what it says – to be with their team constantly, training, motivating, coaching, communicat-

▶

ing, educating, leading: to be visible, giving him or herself totally to their team and managing it holistically. It is *the* full-time aspect of every team leader's daily work.

Cross-functional Management

There is more than a simple expectation in Kaizen companies that projects will be developed from inception cross-functionally – it is a *requirement*. This eliminates problem- or more specifically, solution-myopia and horizons artificially narrowed by the natural constraints bounding any single function.

Assume for a moment that you are project leader of the engineering team responsible for designing and building the passenger doors for a new aeroplane. What other functions would you involve from the beginning and as the project develops? This was the question posed within Boeing as they planned their new 777. Now think about a project unfolding in your own company, and compare who is involved in that with the team eventually put together at Boeing's plant. This involved the door engineers, airframe, fuselage and wing engineers, flight-deck technicians, safety and evacuation specialists, plus personnel managers, technical and cabin crew trainers, marketeers and salespeople. This is what I mean by a cross-functional approach.

Just-in-Time Management

JIT is the production scheduling and pull-through inventory control system developed into its current form by Taiichi Ohno at Toyota. Simply, its aims are threefold: first, to eliminate waste associated with any activity ('waste' is defined as anything which does not add value to quality, hence customer satisfaction); second, to reduce or eliminate expensive stockpiles of parts or finished goods; and third, to ensure that whenever and wherever stock (raw materials or customer-ready products) is required it will be available immediately before its use ie 'just-in-time'.

Kanban

At its simplest, Kanban is a manual reordering system. ('Kanban' translates roughly as 'reorder card'.) MacDonald's restaurants operate a Kanban system: each time the penultimate burger is taken from the chute a numbered stainless steel marker is placed behind the last burger to notify the cooks that there is only one left. Stationery shops frequently operate a Kanban process; again, a reorder marker, often a simple card, is placed between the penultimate and last item which, when exposed, tells an assistant to reorder stock. In the UK cheque books contain a Kanban slip about five cheques before the final one, though most banks and building societies now operate an automatic cheque book resupply system triggered when an assistant keys in a particular cheque number as he or she clears it. This is an electronic Kanban process. Supermarkets operate electronic Kanban systems driven by the bar code on each package.

The purpose of every Kanban system is to activate the next supply station up-stream of the initiator.

Statistical Process Control

Though the forms of analysis used in SPC fall outside the scope of this book, Statistical Process Control is based on relatively simple fundamental principles. Essentially, SPC says that any production process can exhibit two types of variation to the design specification:

- *'Natural' or 'Unassigned' variations* – so-called because there is no identifiable or specific cause of them. They arise within the process itself and, assuming that the process actually is capable of reproducing the precise specification or that the variation is within prescribed tolerances, need not necessarily mean having to change the process.
- *'Assigned' variations* – so-called because they are due to a specific cause, such as a worn cutting tool, a misadjusted lathe, a mis-directed Kanban card.

SPC involves process operators periodically sampling the quality of their own outputs and, using elementary probability theory, deciding for themselves when to shut down the process *before* it produces products which continuously fall outside acceptable quality standards.

The PDCA Cycle

The PDCA Cycle is an endless improvement cycle, which demands of each team that it Plans (looks forward, identifies, understands), Does (takes appropriate and relevant action), Checks (monitors and evaluates effects) and Acts (generating feedback for up-stream teams.)

At each stage action is consolidated, standardized and built into current processes, thus continuously raising standards thresholds. The next PDCA cycle will then unfold.

There are other instruments in Kaizen's tool box, which are each relevant to any of the main instruments outlined above. These include:

- brainstorming
- fishbone analyses
- Pareto analyses
- histograms and scatter (dia)grams
- checklists and tick charts.

Of paramount importance in Kaizen is leadership, both from the very top and of teams. The ability of all leaders, but particularly team leaders (or supervisors, in Western terms), to involve every employee in the Kaizen way of organizational life is critical to maintaining commitment to quality and its continuous improvement. Let me amplify the very particular skills that Kaizen team leaders must possess. (Later, I will highlight the skills that strategic leaders use to underscore their 'visionary' role.)

KAIZEN TEAM LEADERSHIP SKILLS

A Kaizen team leader will be primarily a coach, communicator, trainer, motivator and a resource which his or her team can use to intercede with senior management on its behalf.

A team leader will be more concerned with 'how' his or her team works, rather than exclusively with 'what' it produces. In other words, in the case of the quality of an individual's outputs failing to meet standards, or the team's performance overall falling below par, the leader will painstakingly track back to find the *root* cause. Whether failure to meet a standard is due to a problem in an employee's private life or, say, due to a process weakness, lack of training, lack of motivation, lack of raw materials or lack of communication, it is incumbent upon a Kaizen team leader to answer the questions What? and Why? Even if the answer concerns only one individual in the team, the leader could involve the whole team in identifying the best solution. This approach underscores the family nature of a team, and that none of its mem-

改

bers will be sidelined and left to rely on their own coping mechanisms.

Clearly, a leader's skills have to suit such a human-centred role and their job description will reflect the Kaizen process-oriented approach to leadership. The most important competencies are an understanding of human nature and the needs of people at work, together with an ability to communicate, train, coach, counsel and motivate, as well as represent the company's vision and values in their personal conduct. Naturally, a team leader will be tasked with achieving certain quotas, improvements and, as I mentioned earlier, contributory ideas to their company's suggestion system; but these will be expressed more in terms of his or her responsibility to encourage the team to achieve the quantitative outputs and qualitative standards than in terms of a responsibility for achieving objectives personally. In other words, a Kaizen team leader will focus his or her attention on people primarily and results secondarily – by and large the reverse of a Western supervisor's job.

In summary, then, a team leader in a Kaizen company in the West:

- strengthens teams as the fundamental building blocks of corporate structure
- blends the positive aspects of (Western) individualism with the advantages of team consensus
- focuses on the detail of implementing the big, corporate picture
- acknowledges their personal responsibility to always identify the root cause of problems

- builds strong interpersonal relationships
- leads the drive to improve constantly
- keeps an open mind to constructive criticism and advice
- maintains a progressive, forward-looking attitude
- is willing (and trained) to take responsibility
- takes pride in and reward from his or her team's performance
- challenges received wisdom and supports innovation and creativity.

Clearly, a *team* leader's skills are, by definition, people-centred. The competencies required by those at the top, the *strategists*, are, as you would expect, organization-centred, though not exclusively so. In outline, I would say that a competent company leader must be able to:

- create the vision
- define (qualitatively and quantitatively) the strategy, based on a solid grasp of the objectives, market forces and available resources, and a thorough understanding of strengths, weaknesses, current performance and potential performance
- establish professional standards of performance, and invest the time and effort to communicate them and motivate others to adhere to them
- delegate authority, freedom and resources to the lower-level leaders who will be responsible for implementing the strategy at points of operational action
- lead collective management processes that support

collaboration, co-operation and consultation

- establish and rely upon information feedback systems that are both advisory and sharing in nature

- create the superstructure of success by assigning roles and goals with due regard to balance, task ability and preference, and corporate alignment

- recruit and train the right people, and unify organic strengths.

ROBERT RILEY

Eighty-eight years after Cesar Ritz opened his *de luxe* hotel in London's Piccadilly, Robert Riley took over the management reins on behalf of the hotel's co-owner with Trafalgar House, Hong Kong Land – a part of the Jardine empire and a sister company to the Mandarin Oriental group, itself the owner of some of the world's best hotels.

Riley cut his hotelier's teeth with Mandarin, following careers in law with the New York firm Davis Polk Wardwell, property (including hotel) development in Texas and California and the Ford Foundation working on minority economic and urban redevelopment programmes. His task at Mandarin was to help the group expand, as well as learn to run outstanding hotels whose reputation for excellence had to be protected under intense competitive pressures. His job at the Ritz, which he took on in May 1994, is to restore that hotel's reputation as a luxurious *experience* from its previous somewhat faded glory.

His skill in leadership comes from investing time in under-standing people management – managing large numbers of people in a high profile service industry is neither for the faint hearted nor those who cannot inspire by personal example of confidence, knowledge, fairness and a willingness to share power by pushing down tactical responsibilities. Riley challenges others to think and act creatively – laterally – and he expects to be challenged by those around him.

Riley's warm and friendly persona belies a tough approach to business; he has immense stamina, tenacity, a huge intellect, great powers of focus and a readiness to embrace change as an environmental factor here to stay. He drives himself and his people hard, but not at the expense of quality and his human resource.

Uppermost is his insistence that his employees have the resources to continuously surprise and delight his hotels' customers. Overall, he sees people as his business's greatest asset. Managing the Mandarin group strategically – he is responsible for eight Mandarin hotels – is as stimulating as finding out at first hand what impact his plans are having on those right down the command chain who have to translate his vision into dollar-earning action.

Yet despite his bruising work schedule he believes firmly in achieving a balance between his business and family lives; and he encourages everyone to manage a harmony between all their interests – work, home, spiritual and civic.

In addition, Kaizen leaders must be the embodiment of the Kaizen philosophy, best summed up in the single word *harmony*. To the Japanese, harmony has traditionally been a sublime quality, the pinnacle of personal achievement and a demonstration of inner strength and self-confidence. To be in

改

harmony with one's colleagues, company, products and, indeed, nature and the whole of life is good; to be antagonistic, confrontational, belligerent, impolite, even angry is to be weak and to lose face. This in turn demonstrates loss of respect for oneself and the other person; it displaces harmony with dissonance and a blame culture. And the Japanese believe that in a blame culture, where there is little respect for individuals (whether fellow employees, suppliers or customers) there will be little trust, little openness, little honesty and, therefore, an environment in which it can be impossible to admit mistakes, share resources and achieve a resolution – an improvement – quickly and inexpensively.

To us in the West 'harmony', as it is aspired to in Japan, can be expressed in quite flowery and poetical language. It is, however, a deadly serious pursuit. Konosuke Matsushita, for example, favoured these guidelines for his global electrical conglomerate: 'Happiness of man is built on mental stability and material affluence. To serve the foundation of happiness, through making man's life affluent with an inexpensive and inexhaustible supply of necessities like water inflow, is the duty of the manufacturer. Profit comes in compensation for contribution to society. If the enterprise tries to earn a reasonable profit but fails to do so, it is because the degree of its social contribution is still insufficient.' Matsushita's 'Seven Spiritual (company) Values' spring from this embracing concept of harmony: 1 National service through industry; 2 Fairness; 3 Harmony and co-operation; 4 Struggle for betterment; 5 Courtesy and humility; 6 Adjustment and assimilation; 7 Gratitude.

Harmony is a core value in Kaizen and, while it sounds an alien quality to Western business leaders, its power for the good should never be underestimated nor dismissed as Asian mysticism. As Masaaki Imai, a foremost proponent of Kaizen, said in his seminal book, *Kaizen: The Key to Japan's Competitive Success**:

> 'A confrontation between (Japanese and Western) cultures (will) be avoided if you acknowledge the fact that Kaizen will succeed or fail in your organization not for reasons of nationality but of mentality.'

Respect for individuals can be summed up like this:

Respect for individuals

1   Each individual must value and respect every other individual, not just those in their own department or at their own level.

2   Respect means believing that every individual has the innate capacity to spot areas for improvement anywhere in their company, not just in their own work area.

3   Each individual should be sufficiently confident in themself and their team colleagues (including the team's leader) to openly admit personal errors or weaknesses/failings in the job process(es) for which they are responsible, without fear of negative repercussions. This is being in harmony.

---

*Kaizen: The Key to Japan's Competitive Success by Masaaki Imai [McGraw Hill 1986]. Masaaki Imai, Chairman of the Kaizen Institute, has played a major role in promoting Kaizen throughout the world.

改

4   Everyone must believe that progress is impossible without the ability to own up to mistakes; but, by the same token, everyone must accept a personal responsibility to learn from mistakes to re-establish harmony and standards.

5   Respecting individuals contains the implicit injunction that individuals must respect their company (the company is its people, after all). This means everyone must be(come) involved in company life and feel an obligation to help the company achieve its production, quality and delivery standards.

6   Respect for individuals means working cross-functionally with no protectionism or proprietoriality of one's own department, nor of information. (Information, or knowledge, is not a route to power in a Kaizen company.)

In this environment it is quite possible to believe that the following story actually happened, rather than it being just apocryphal. A cupboard door kept swinging open. (In a traditional Western company someone would be asked to close it; after a while they would tire of doing it and ask someone else; this person too would get fed up with having to close the constantly open door until, eventually, either someone called in a repairman to fix a replacement catch or the open door is allowed to become part of the scenery.) In the Kaizen company in this story, an employee decided to find out why the door would not stay closed. He examined the cupboard's handles, hinges, construction and locking mechanism, dismantling each down to its component units. The employee involved his work team colleagues in a total assessment of the quality of each component unit and, subsequently, the redesign of certain parts and sub-assemblies. These were pre-

sented to the cupboard manufacturer. That company con-
tacted its component suppliers, who incorporated the user's
new designs, thus eradicating the reason for the swinging
door.

Such attention to preventative rather than symptomatic
detail is the very stuff of Kaizen, as is the attitude that making
do and accepting things as they are is simply not good
enough. It would have been very easy to fix a replacement
catch or a new set of hinges, but that would not have
answered the question, *Why* did the door not stay closed?
Had the door not been a door on an inconsequential office
cupboard but, say, the window winder on a car the Kaizen
attitude would have saved British Leyland huge loss of face
(plus loss of business and terrible publicity) when, in the
1970s at a time when Toyota was designing a new breed of
car and offering virtually unconditional quality guarantees
with its vehicles, window winders, wing mirrors, rearview
mirrors and other components kept failing on Austin, Rover
and Jaguar vehicles. BL's lack of attention to detail, its appar-
ent disinterest in quality and its lack of motivation to find the
real answers to the question Why? made easy sales for its
competitors. BL's leadership was not solely to blame, but the
debilitating confrontations it found itself having to cope with
could have been averted if both unions and management had
maintained their focus on satisfying customers through producing quality products, and on replacing blame with openness and harmony.

It has been a long journey but Rover (under the aegis of its
partner Honda) and its prime components supplier Unipart
have both used Kaizen to transform company culture and
production processes. Indeed, the turnaround in Britain's car

industry has been one of the success stories of the 1990s and it is no exaggeration to say that Kaizen has been the key to consumers' new-found trust in the quality of British vehicles.

According to the director of America's prestigious Malcolm Baldridge National Quality Award, a company must exhibit eight essential characteristics:

1   A plan to keep improving all operations continuously;

2   A system for measuring these improvements accurately;

3   A strategic plan based on benchmarks that compare the company's performance with the world's best;

4   A close partnership with suppliers and customers that feeds improvements back into the operation;

5   A deep understanding of the customers so that their wants can be translated into products;

6   A long-lasting relationship with customers, going beyond the delivery of the product to include sales, service and ease of maintenance;

7   A focus on preventing mistakes rather than merely correcting them;

8   A commitment to improving quality that runs from the top of the organization to the bottom.

None of this happened by accident. Kaizen was consciously chosen and implemented from the top. Managing a major paradigm break from conventional Western production processes and management style to a culture based on Kaizen (albeit an adapted Kaizen) demands the very strongest and committed leadership – to forge out of the old a new environment in which employees are empowered to make the leadership's vision a reality.

'I believe a good leader, a top leader, will be recognized as such by the organization. But it is something he has to earn by setting the right example. Of course, a top leader should have vision – be able to think and look ahead about what is needed for the future. But it is not only a matter of saying what has to be done, it is also a matter of being seen to be doing it yourself. Only the winning companies will survive and the top leader must have a fierce desire to win. It is this vision and having the ability to follow it through that separates the real leader from the normal manager.'

Gerard van den Akker,
Chairman, Netherland's Export Combination,
winner of the 1991 European Quality Award for Leadership

'The competitive edge will increasingly depend upon the quality, commitment and skills of our employees. Thus, the senior manager will be required to be even more the leader, motivator and moulder of the management team, and will need to ensure the involvement and motivation of all employees in the company's objectives. This is particularly important with the increasing challenge of change – companies will only change quickly if the whole team is involved in understanding the process of change and is backing it.'

Sir Ian Wood,
Chairman and Managing Director,
John Wood Construction Limited

'Management is about getting more out of people than even they believe is in them. I'm talking about inspiring self-belief. A manager's job is to create circumstances in which every indivi-

己久

dual can realize his or her full potential. Managing is about giving people the opportunity to succeed and letting them get on with it.'

Sir Allen Sheppard,
Chairman and Chief Executive, Grand Metropolitan, plc,
winner of the Institute of Management's Gold Medal

These are not the sentiments of weak leaders who lack confidence in themselves or their people. Robert Heller, in his book *Superchiefs*, lists ten criteria for the 'new management'. He writes that leaders of tomorrow's businesses will:

1 Invest to win leadership in the technology of products and process.

2 Give effective power to people with clear responsibility.

3 Train and educate everyone, from top to bottom, all the time.

4 Lead a management collective that collaborates, co-operates and consults.

5 Create the superstructure of success by assigning the right roles to the right people.

6 Use the fullest possible information for the most ambitious possible strategy.

7 Master and develop the new techniques of hard and soft management.

8 Link responsibility, status and rewards to prime performance.

9 Acquire the means of achieving the impossible.

10 Unify organic strengths to win exemplary success.

It is no accident that this list is informed by Kaizen's principles: Kaizen-based companies are among the most powerful in the world (and they are not all Japanese), and those that have chosen to adopt TQM – so closely related to Kaizen – are internally oriented towards employees.

Again and again I meet business leaders who emphasize the importance of understanding and working *with* their workforce to get the best return in the training, education, power and responsibility invested in them. Terms like 'continuous training', 'achieving the impossible', 'trust', and 'sharing' are repeated too frequently to be dismissed as an ideal achievable by only a few (large, multinational) conglomerates which can 'afford to experiment'. The role of a leader and the shape of organizations of *every* size is changing. Gerard van den Akker summed up a great deal of the sentiments I have heard expressed, when he said,

> 'It seems that ten years ago the leader's main function was to make decisions, rightly or wrongly, and direct every level and function of the entire organization's operation. The leader in today's organization, however, involves others in his decision-making process, has "people management" skills, is "people oriented" and ensures that the organization satisfies its customers, shareholders, employees and society.'

KAIZEN IN THE UK

The concept of Kaizen is now reasonably well-established in the UK in large companies, but less so in small and medium-sized businesses.

Percentage of senior managers aware of Kaizen

Large companies   94 per cent

Small/medium size companies   44 per cent

Percentage of senior managers in large companies with experience of Kaizen

Manufacturing sector   88 per cent

Service sector   53 per cent

Source: Europe Japan Centre, *Survey of Japanese Human Resource Practices in the UK (1993)*

Interviews with senior managers in 50 of the leading 250 UK companies suggest that Kaizen is viewed positively. These were the comments most frequently mentioned.

What UK managers said about Kaizen

- It is an extremely powerful concept that has a great deal to offer.

- It is an essential ingredient for future competitiveness.

- It leads to higher quality goods and services.

- It can lead to a more efficient organization.

- It improves business results.

- It helps to eliminate waste

Source: Europe Japan Centre, *Survey of Japanese Human Resource Practices in the UK (1993)*

Although respondents spoke positively about Kaizen, many acknowledged that there were problems with the approach. There are three main concerns.

1 It is difficult to achieve in practice.
2 It is difficult to maintain enthusiasm.

3 Continuous improvement is not sufficient by itself; companies also need major innovations.

Source: Europe Japan Centre, *Survey of Japanese Human Resource Practices in the UK (1993)*

Difficult to achieve

- Requires a complete change in attitude and culture.
- Needs the energy and commitment of all employees.
- Requires a great amount of time.

Difficult to maintain

- Some people see Kaizen as a threat to their jobs.
- A lot of poor ideas are put forward, as well as good ones, which can be demotivating.
- By implication, there is never complete satisfaction.

Innovation also needed

- Sometimes it is better to do things better, but it may not be commercially sensible.
- It can make people blind to the wider issues.
- There is a danger of becoming exclusively evolutionary at the expense of revolutionary advances.

Very few of these problems are insurmountable, particularly if there is commitment by senior managers, as we shall see later.

I am frequently asked how Kaizen can be introduced into a business. Looking at the faces of my questioners, often opinion leaders and powerful people in their own right, I am at

改

one and the same time delighted but cautious. Delighted, because of the very genuine interest in Kaizen and that it is being correctly understood as a powerful galvanizing force that most definitely puts employees at the hub of the corporate dynamic and thus deserving of the renewed and sustained attention I spoke of earlier; cautious, because Kaizen is not a panacea for all ills and neither is it a philosophy that can be introduced either in its textbook-pure form or overnight. On the one hand, Kaizen must be adapted and blended with Western business cultures and Western management theory if it is to stand any chance of being accepted and observed by Western employees, and on the other, it will likely take a large business the better part of ten years before a conventionally-managed Western business can consider itself run totally according to Kaizen's principles.

That said, those companies – large and small, manufacturing and service businesses, in the UK, USA and Europe – which have embraced Kaizen (in the Eastern and Western blend that I recommend) have found the journey challenging, exciting and wholly transforming. They would now never return to the 'old' ways, having experienced the tangible benefits of Kaizen.

To answer the question, I tell business leaders there are four key requirements that, whilst not *guaranteeing* success will guarantee failure if not observed.

THE REQUIREMENTS FOR SUCCESS
WITH KAIZEN

- Senior management commitment is essential.

- Senior managers must be clear of Kaizen's role in the overall business strategy.

- All employees should understand Kaizen's role in their work.

- Kaizen should be linked to personal development and enablement.

Senior management's commitment

In Japan, the cultural background means that senior management commitment is usually taken for granted. Local guidelines therefore concentrate on shopfloor involvement. In the UK, where the cultural background is different, ensuring the right management commitment is essential.

Senior managers need to understand Kaizen and how it fits into the company's overall strategy. They should also be aware of the implications and potential disruptions that the introduction of Kaizen will bring:

- reorganizing of people into teams takes time and may be disruptive

- training and group meetings take additional time

- productivity may decline temporarily while changes are implemented

- some employees may be suspicious and unco-operative.

These problems can be overcome, but managers need to be aware of them and spend time dealing with them, rather than abandoning Kaizen before it has a chance to yield positive results. The programme must be sustained by personal enthusiasm and commitment.

Kaizen's Role in the Overall Business Strategy

Managers should not be so enthusiastic about Kaizen that they neglect the wider issues of planning for major growth by innovation, as well as by gradual improvement. The introduction of Kaizen should free senior managers to think about the long-term future of their business, look for new opportunities and concentrate on strategic issues. Kaizen will support the improvement of existing activities, but it will not provide the impetus for the great leap forward. It is vital to retain the balance between Western innovation and individual creativity and Kaizen's focus on improvement.

Employees' Role in Kaizen

Different attitudes to employment in the UK means that, initially, Kaizen may not be perceived as a positive benefit. The fear is that people may improve themselves out of a job or be asked to do more work for no additional reward.

Companies such as Rover, influenced by their co-operation with Honda, have made employment commitments to their workforce. It is essential to stress the positive benefits of Kaizen, showing how improvements in productivity and quality should lead to growth of the business in other directions. Managers should also consider how the benefits of Kaizen can be passed on in the form of financial or other rewards.

Linking Kaizen to Personal Development

Traditionally, Kaizen programmes have not placed sufficient emphasis on personal development. Companies have concentrated on processes and systems rather than developing and tapping the creativity of all employees.

The success of Kaizen depends so much on attitudes and enthusiasm that time and money must be invested in training. Leaders therefore need to get close to their people, to share the vision of the future and to encourage them to develop their own goals in line with that vision. They must ensure that their company's human resource policy encourages people to contribute positively. They must develop working patterns that enable people to use their skills in the most effective way through teamwork and an atmosphere of collaboration.

The leaders of tomorrow's businesses will develop organizations that can win in global markets through innovative company strategies and higher quality products and services. To achieve the required degree of flexibility and speed of response, leaders have no option but to decentralize decision-making and give their people the authority and freedom to contribute – leaders simply cannot do it all themselves: they cannot be everywhere at once and, however experienced and skilled they are, there are too many forces and risks involved in business today for the choice to be left to one person. I remember once visiting a medium-sized company in the UK and asking the managing director what he enjoyed doing most. He looked rather sheepish and then replied, 'What I really enjoy is opening all the post in the morning.' If he spends his time opening the post, who, I wondered, spends their time on strategy?

This much you already know, I am sure; yet it constantly amazes me how little leaders in business open doors to their workforces so that they can contribute. Too few leaders either trust their employees or believe that, unless they work at a certain level and carry a particular title they have anything to contribute. I have to remind them of one of Kaizen's fundamental tenets that *every* employee has the innate capacity (and in the majority of cases the desire) to add new ideas, new perspectives, new thinking to any given process.

It is clear that companies must become more flexible – by making more efficient use of human resources – to succeed in demonstrably competitive markets, where the greatest force for change is consumers' wants. (Leaders seem to forget that each one of their employees is a consumer and, if they were but asked, could tell the company why its products or services succeed or fail.)

I spoke earlier of 'organizational integration'; involving employees is part of the process of achieving this. Achieving flexibility and the right internal dynamic comes from creating an 'agile organization', capable of competing successfully both domestically and internationally.

THE AGILE ORGANIZATION

- Requires people who are flexible and capable of co-ordinating action effectively in the midst of permanent change and uncertainty.
- Values creativity and flexibility.
- Emphasizes teamwork over individualism.
- Focuses on customers, not short-term profit.
- May seek global rather than just domestic markets.

- Brings out totally new products and services quickly.

- Assimilates field experience and technological innovation, continually modifying and improving its products and services.

- Produces to order.

- Measures quality by assessing customer satisfaction over the full life of the product or service.

- Continuously invests in the skill base of its employees because they are valued as the company's prime resource.

- Acknowledges that the workforce is responsible for innovation, product and service evolution, and for production process improvements.

- Integrates technology, management and the workforce into a co-ordinated, interdependent system.

These shifts in context (from what I call 'non-Kaizen' to 'Kaizen' or, if you prefer, 'agility') suggest the challenges facing managers. Even though no individual shift is beyond coping, the collective impact (and implications) of the whole cluster imposes a burden under which a traditional approach to organisational and human resource management would collapse.

The shift in managerial style can be summarized like this:

From	*To*
- Hierarchy	- Networks and flatness
- Linear, sequential problem solving	- Parallel and simultaneous problem solving

- Vertical tasks within functional units

- Content

- Absolute truth based on inflexible laws and principles

- Managers leading and workers following

- Single techniques

- Companies as machines in which there is emphasis on the 'hard Ss': strategy, structure and systems

- Horizontal tasks and collaboration across functions

- Process

- Dynamic approximations based on ambiguity and paradox

- Facilitation and employees empowered to innovate and initiate change

- Holistic synthesis (see panel below)

- Companies as organisms in which there is emphasis on the 'soft Ss': style, staff and shared values

---

HOLISTIC SYNTHESIS

Synthesis is very important in Kaizen organizations, and is crucial in conventional Western companies embarking on the transition from traditional to the Eastern/Western blend I advocate. It was the nineteenth-century German philosopher Georg Hegel who introduced the concept of 'a synthesis of opposites'. His notion was that when one argument (which he called a 'thesis') is juxtaposed with its counter-argument (which he called the 'antithesis') a new case (the 'synthesis') which both includes and transcends the original constituents – and which can be a stronger argument – can arise. Some simple examples illustrate this:

Thesis	*Antithesis*	*Synthesis*
Yes	No	Perhaps
Black	White	Grey
Non-Kaizen	Kaizen	A blend of East and West
Plan A	Plan B	Incremental transformation

The Ford Motor Company used this approach in the late 1970s/early 1980s to foster adaptation and continuous learning, to take the company away from its traditions and develop in its managers new mindsets:

The Process at Ford

Thesis	*Antithesis*	*Synthesis*
Rigidly planned	Opportunistic	Strategic opportunism
Hierarchical élitism	Egalitarian pluralism	Interdependent 'superstars'
Mandatory rules	Discretionary behaviour	Regulated latitude
Managerial control	Freedom	Enlightened discipline
Hard minds	Soft hearts	Compassionate pragmatism
Maximize results	Maximize process	Evolving excellence

This table, adapted from Richard Pascale's *Managing on the Edge*, illustrates how Ford developed and enhanced pre-existing organizational strengths and employee competencies, introduced new frameworks around which new and old values were interwoven, drew on the entire organization to drive the change, and succeeded without 'throwing the baby out with the bath water'. Of course, Ford had the will to change and were

▶

prepared to invest time, money and effort to achieve a new culture. Without these prerequisites, the exercise could have been hollow and an exercise in artifice. As it was, the thesis – antithesis – synthesis process was powerfully transforming. By the beginning of the 1990s Ford had evolved this simply-worded but precise vision and values statement:

Ford's Vision and Values

Mission

Ford Motor Company is a worldwide leader in automotive and automotive-related products and services as well as in newer industries such as aerospace, communications, and financial services. Our mission is to improve continually our products and services to meet our customers' needs, allowing us to prosper as a business and to provide a reasonable return for our stockholders, the owners of our business.

Values

How we accomplish our mission is as important as the mission itself. Fundamental to success for the Company are these basic values:

- *People* – Our people are the source of our strength. They provide our corporate intelligence and determine our reputation and vitality. Involvement and teamwork are our core human values.

- *Products* – Our products are the end result of our efforts, and they should be the best in serving customers worldwide. As our products are viewed, so are we viewed.

- *Profits* – Profits are the ultimate measure of how efficiently we provide customers with the best products for their needs. Profits are required to survive and grow.

Guiding Principles

- *Quality comes first* – To achieve customer satisfaction, the quality of our products and services must be our number one priority.

- *Customers are the focus of everything we do* – Our work must be done with our customers in mind, providing better products and services than our competition.

- *Continous improvement is essential to our success* – We must strive for excellence in everything we do: our products, in their safety and value – and in our services, our human relations, our competitiveness, and our profitability.

- *Employee involvement is our way of life* – We are a team. We must treat each other with trust and respect.

- *Dealers and suppliers are our partners* – The company must maintain mutually beneficial relationships with dealers, suppliers, and our other business associates.

- *Integrity is never compromised* – The conduct of our Company worldwide must be pursued in a manner that is socially responsible and commands respect for its integrity and for its positive contributions to society. Our doors are open to men and women alike without discrimination and without regard to ethnic origin or personal beliefs.

Developing this integration and agility has been a key step in the survival of the West's automotive industry, for many years the Cinderella of our manufacturing base. In more cases than not, survival, rebirth and growth has been the consequence of new leadership based on the Kaizen model. Two histories, those of General Motors and European Components, illustrate my point:

GENERAL MOTORS

GM's plant at Fremont, California, suffered from one of the worst labour relations records in GM; low productivity, low morale and, as a consequence, poor quality products.

Yet, just two years after it reopened under Toyota leadership and management in a joint venture with General Motors, the plant received international acclaim for its world-class quality and productivity and its harmonious labour relations. The success of the transformation was not due to wholesale sackings or anti-union activities – the new company employed around 85 per cent of the same workforce and union officials as before.

The difference was the new spirit of consensus and trust. The new company, known as New United Motor Manufacturing INC (NUMMI), and the key union, United Auto Workers, pledged to replace traditional adversarial bargaining with joint problem solving by both parties, seeking opportunities for mutual gain while building a climate of good faith and trust. At the heart of the agreement was an acceptance that both parties agreed to share all the risk, responsibility and rewards of partnership. This in turn was based on a shared vision: '*Together we can build the best subcompact cars in the world.*'

The spirit of the agreement was embodied in seven goals that reflected 'new management' attitudes:

1 Constant improvement through Kaizen.
2 Develop full human potential.
3 Pursuit of superior quality.
4 Build mutual trust.
5 Develop team performance.
6 Every employee is a manager.
7 Provide a stable livelihood.

Supporting these goals is a flat, democratic organization built on functional teams from bottom to top. These provide a framework for continuous collaborative problem-solving. By regularly involving all parties affected by a problem and using solutions reached by consensus, the company improves understanding of the problem and increases the commitment of everyone to the solution.

Effectively, this means that NUMMI employs problem-solving 'leaders' throughout the organization. Here, the emerging view of employees is that they are 'partners' rather than 'hired hands'. To ensure that each can perform their new role effectively, NUMMI invested considerable money, time and effort in training and development. Without that, employee empowerment would have been an empty concept.

Another example of the successful use of Kaizen principles is European Components.

EUROPEAN COMPONENTS

European Components, a subsidiary of the Japanese Takata Corporation, manufactures components for the European car industry on two sites in Belfast, Northern Ireland. The automotive components market is a classic example of a global marketplace in which manufacturers source from the suppliers who can achieve best of class in cost, quality and delivery.

The company took a fundamental decision that none of the Kaizen tools and techniques was to be used for any process unless it supported the company's overall objective – to be number one in Europe. A number of five-year objectives were set:

▶

- 30 per cent market share

- Zero defects in all activities

- Factory costs equivalent to 75 per cent of sales

- Improved internal and external communications.

Departmental objectives

The company used an approach called 'policy deployment' to turn its overall business objectives into meaningful departmental objectives.

1 Each department's responsibilities were established in relation to the overall corporate objective.
2 Departments were set one-year objectives. Performance against standards was to be assessed monthly.
3 Detailed improvements were specified on monthly assessment forms for each item, and training was established to help people meet those objectives. Any problems in performance were detailed in monthly meetings for all managers.

European Components believe that there are a number of factors crucial to the success of Kaizen in their company:

- *Planning* – Planning is essential to identifying the activities that need to be improved. They believe that Japanese managers spend up to 80 per cent of their time planning, while European managers spend 80 per cent of their time acting.

- *Good housekeeping* – This ensures a safe, pleasant and efficient working environment. It also provides a good first impression for new customers visiting the plant.

- *Leadership* – Kaizen gives a focus to everything in the company, so it is important that senior managers are committed to its success.

- *Patience* – Kaizen is not a quick fix. It is hundreds of thousands of small changes; it is important, therefore, that people do not expect too much too soon. European Components' employees understand that steady, progressive evolution, rather than revolution, will ensure the company achieves its five-year goals without compromising its values or jeopardising either its internal processes or the quality of its products. Like companies in Japan, European Components is learning to take the long view, at the expense of making a quick buck.

Both these companies are fully-integrated organizations: the 'glue' that holds them together is Kaizen; they, too, are agile organizations: despite the consensus approach to decision-making, which undeniably takes longer than in the past, the market and customer research undertaken is more sound, the planning is more rigorous and complete, the actions are therefore more confident, the environments are rich in terms of ideas, suggestions and creativity, and the teams are so flexible that both companies can respond quickly to market trends by constantly improving existing products to reflect consumers' wants rather than having to build from scratch each time the opportunity pendulum swings one way and then the other.

In a nutshell, the success of both these companies is based on Kaizen's powerful unifying cultural force, committed leadership and an insistence that internal processes be perfect. One of Kaizen's maxims is, get the *processes* right (training, leadership, team, communication, inter-relationship, manufacturing, cost and waste control, performance measurement, distribution processes) and the wanted outcomes (quality products, customer satisfaction, market share, profit) will follow as an inevitable consequence. This is a message I keep emphasizing at seminars and to those company leaders who are actively considering adopting Kaizen. It highlights one of the marked differences between Kaizen and non-Kaizen organizations; in the latter, results tend to be everything – how they are achieved appears to have been given less consideration during the past decade. This, of course, reflects Western managements' preference for action (frequently action for survival) rather than planning. In Kaizen companies the reverse is the rule: plan, plan and replan before acting, and ensure the processes are right for the tasks. If the planning is right, the people are right and the processes are right there can be only one outcome.

This is good theory; it cannot be faulted. But it is this very emphasis on developing processes and a company's people that makes introducing Kaizen into Western businesses a long affair. This in turn demands exceptionally strong, focused and committed leadership to ensure no drift from the goal. European Components first introduced Kaizen something over five years ago. They say they are still learning and have some way to go to complete the paradigm shift. Unipart, once a wholly-owned subsidiary of British Leyland during the turbulent 1970s, introduced Kaizen some ten years ago after privatizing and because of the influence exerted by the then Austin Rover Group and its later joint venture partner,

Honda. Unipart, too, are still learning, but as John Neill, Unipart's chief executive, has said, 'Constantly learning is part of the philosophy of constant improvement: there is no end to either; there is no target that once reached means that as an organization we can stop improving our products or the processes used to make them or, as employees we can stop acquiring new knowledge and new skills.'

What Neill and his team leaders are practising is self-referencing; that is, as Kaizen advocates improvement via constant small-step, evolutionary improvements, it should be introduced in the same way – a process of slow but sure, steadily advancing change away from conventional Western business practices and towards a blend of Western and Eastern. Steering the change and maintaining the momentum are the leaders' tasks.

SUMMARY

Tomorrow's businesses will look very different internally from those with us today. The emphasis on retooling, whether this means new machinery or computer-assisted administrative and training systems (including virtual reality design and personal training programmes), will continue – investment in electronic technology has really only just started – but it will be matched, if not eclipsed, by major employee development and employee management programmes.

These will be the consequence of new corporate values that will underpin the importance of the workforce to company success. In their turn, the values will be based on a new culture that eschews closed communities at work and recognizes the benefits of sharing information, localizing decision making, training constantly, communicating fully, and opening-up the company to make it more transparent and accountable to its stakeholders.

Traditional styles of leadership will change to satisfy the bottom-up demand for equality of opportunities to shape company affairs; and leaders will be markedly more process oriented than the emphasis on results has allowed them to be in the past.

Overall, the most significantly felt difference will be the *inclusivity* of *all* employees in the total company dynamic – to express it somewhat crudely, they will have *their* hands on the company, rather than the company having its hands on them, in a wholly shared effort to fulfil business objectives.

I was reminded a day or so ago of some work I did with a management consultancy in 1993 to help them achieve high team performance through participatory and consensus leadership.

CONSULTANCY

On the left are the reasons I found why this particular consultancy was failing to gain better market advantage from its highly competent professional employees; on the right are the Kaizen approaches I used to first, *deconstruct* old behaviours and second, build a strong, interdependent unit that gave to its members the involvement, determinism and local control that overcame the barriers to performance that had existed.

Why the team did not perform	The Kaizen solution
• Imbalance between project contributors and project tasks	Rebalancing by assigning project roles and goals according to individual strengths and performances (*See* Chapter 2).
• Ingrained individualism and strong interpersonal competitiveness	A strategic requirement to collaborate cross-functionally and to change proprietorial information (knowledge) from a route to personal power to shared information as a route to corporate efficiency and market competitiveness.
• Scapegoating	Elimination of the blame culture and its replacement by one in which problems are admitted openly and resolved collectively, thus creating a learning environment.
• Projects developed and managed in a corporate vacuum	Leaders developed to communicate corporate vision and objectives down through the hierarchy and to process feedback up through the hierarchy to them, where lessons could be incorporated in flexed business plans.
• Lack of integration between sub-teams	Cross-functional communication, job/team

改

▶

	rotations and training for leaders in influencing skills, coaching skills, team management skills and the development of control trusteeship.
• Lack of 'real participation' in the company	Replacement of Chinese walls with a matrix of open communication channels, and additional training for leaders in *boundary* management.
• Autocracy	The development of 'adhocracy' and corporate values that prize 'democratic entrepreneurship'.

2

WHAT WILL BE THE ROLE OF TOMORROW'S LEADERS?

改善

INTRODUCTION

I painted an overview picture in chapter 1 of 'tomorrow's businesses' being more 'open book', internally and externally accountable, egalitarian and employee-centred than the majority are today.

In them, a top-down cascade of information, strategic plans and vision-inspired leadership will meet a bottom-up fountain of contributory ideas, team-sponsored decisions, tactical implementation activities and mentored self-development in an open-arena environment criss-crossed by a network of communication channels that reach out to suppliers and customers and draw everyone together in a partnership relationship.

The amount of information that will be generated (by extensive and more frequent market and customer research surveys) and made available to staff will not only be of an order of magnitude greater than now, it will be absolutely necessary to ensure that everyone understands their company's aims, its markets, changes in the environmental forces impacting its position and products, and how trading in both threat and opportunity times will be sustained. In addition, information will have to be shared up and downstream to ensure the right decisions and value judgments are made *in context*. Education and training for staff is therefore a pre-requisite to help them analyze and make sense of in-bound data, and then use it competently to benefit personal and team performances.

In the flatter organizations of tomorrow, in which whole layers which once provided stages in career progress and pro-motion have been stripped out, task enrichment, multi-skilling, job rotation/job sharing and giving the responsibility to employees for their own development will feature as important means of maintaining motivation, morale and loyalty.

As power and authority are disseminated employees will need to feel that senior management has sufficient confidence in them – and, importantly, *in themselves* – to give them the freedom, or empowerment, to work with minimal manage-rial supervision. Management by exception will characterize this hands-off approach, and as managers step back from day-to-day operational detail – leaving this to team leaders while they fulfil their strategic management responsibilities – per-formance monitoring, appraising and disciplining procedures will become peer owned and operated, frequently becoming two-way, in which 'interviewer' and 'interviewee' participate in 360° reviews simultaneously.

Looking at my sentiments here, based on the practices within Kaizen and Kaizen-influenced companies, it is clear that a leader's role will become increasingly one that can be encapsulated in the responsibility for first, implemen-ting what I call the *enablement equation* and second, team management.

THE ENABLEMENT EQUATION

To many opinion leaders with whom I speak the enablement equation is *the* most potent symbol of Kaizen and the responsibilities which this business culture imposes on a leader.

The enablement equation is expressed like this:

- when an employee does not know what to do . . . *communicate*
- when an employee does not know how to do it . . . *train*
- when an employee does not want to do it . . . *motivate*
- when an employee knows what to do, is competent and is motivated to do it . . . *empower*
- when an employee has done it and meets (or exceeds) standards . . . *reward.*

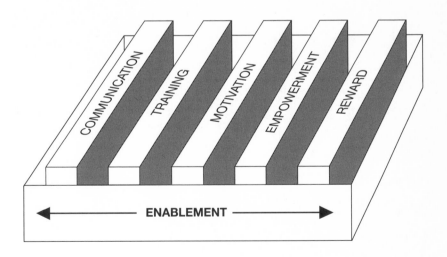

改

These five components – communication, training, motivation, empowerment and reward – express the core skills in which Kaizen leaders must be fully competent. They are the subjects most featured in the extensive job training that Kaizen leaders receive. They are skills which are too important to be left to chance. So let me amplify each of them for you here.

Communication

Kaizen leaders sit at the nodes of the communication nexus within their company. They are communication gatekeepers of fundamental importance to the free-flow of communication, responsible for originating, receiving, interpreting, presenting, channelling and managing information and the communication paths to and from their teams.

Naturally, as information is openly shared – information is not the source of personal power in a Kaizen organization and thus to be held on to, but the source of team and company efficiency, and thus to be eagerly sought and distributed – the nexus is transparent and fully two-way: feedback is an inseparable part of interpersonal and interteam communication, and no-one is immune from an appraisal of both their ability to communicate well and the information that they communicate.

I must emphasize the critical nature of Kaizen teamleaders' communication role: on the one hand, they will be expected (following appropriate training) to be able to read, understand and re-present to their team members market and customer research analyses, profit and loss statements, trading reports, production records, etc. – in both text and diagram formats; and on the other, to participate in feedback sessions, where any character flaw will show itself and be a potential weakness in the communication process. This role, though not necessarily more so than the others in the enablement equation, strongly highlights the *task* and *psychological* competencies which a leader must possess to function effectively in an open and team-based community where, particularly in *Western* Kaizen companies, a leader who lacks personal confidence and personal power cannot hide behind rank or positional authority. I remind the people with whom I talk about Kaizen that self-criticism in front of one's peers and subordinates is part of the cultural history common to Far Eastern societies and, although Kaizen companies in the West do not go in for such soul-baring sessions (any more than they go in for *Tai Chi* or early morning company songs and workouts), the spirit of such openness undeniably underscores the expected conduct of leaders.

Although individuality is more prized in the West than the East, most Kaizen leaders share common personality traits:

A Kaizen Leader's Mindset

The ideal Kaizen leader is:

- open-minded
- able to conceptualize
- intelligent, and able and willing to learn new behaviours
- team-oriented
- flexible and adaptable
- self-disciplined and self-motivated

改

- a first-class communicator of ideas
- loyal to his or her team and their company
- responsive to his or her own leaders
- perceptually attentive.

Kaizen leaders, I must stress, are not 'tame' psychologists, there for the emotional benefit of the workforce, though understanding human nature and counselling when it is appropriate to do so *are* key tools in their bag of competencies. Both during a transition to an Eastern plus Western organization culture and once that culture is self-sustaining, they should never lose sight of their pure output-related responsibilities. However, whilst these task-related functions – a *results* focus, if you like – will be quite familiar to all leaders (they are, after all, *the* key performance indicator most common amongst traditional Western companies), it is the change to 'small, autonomous units (teams), organizing downwards, switching from bureaucracy to "adhocracy", reframing from hierarchical separatism to flexible cross-functionalism and the will to commit to long-term plans (rather than short-termism)', as Robert Waterman says in his latest book *Frontiers of Excellence*, that will test the sheer staying power of tomorrow's leaders. The psychological demands on them, requiring a willing release of total command and control, matching attention to the bottom line with an equal attention to people, allowing more self-direction (and self-directed teams) and understanding that nothing comes first, everything and everyone should be organizationally integrated in a strategic partnership, can require a fundamental shift in what Western leaders have grown up with and been trained in. For older managers and supervisors the attitudinal change can be big, and tough to make.

The point that I am coming to is that leaders themselves, though responsible for implementing the enablement equation with their people, will likely need just the same from their own leaders. They, too, need information (clear and timely communication) and training; this is the second part of the enablement equation.

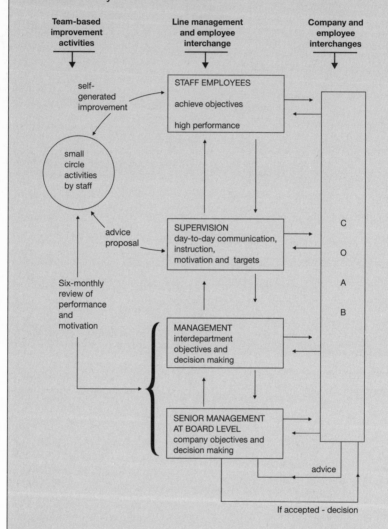

TOSHIBA CONSUMER PRODUCTS

This outline diagram depicts the two-way flow of communication traffic laterally and vertically within Toshiba Consumer Products at Plymouth in the UK.

Team-based improvement activities

Line management and employee interchange

Company and employee interchanges

self-generated improvement

STAFF EMPLOYEES
achieve objectives
high performance

small circle activities by staff

advice proposal

SUPERVISION
day-to-day communication,
instruction,
motivation and targets

C

O

Six-monthly review of performance and motivation

A

B

MANAGEMENT
interdepartment
objectives and
decision making

SENIOR MANAGEMENT
AT BOARD LEVEL
company objectives and
decision making

advice

If accepted - decision

Note: 'COAB' stands for Company Advisory Board, a forum in which TCP employees, managers, team leaders, union officers and executives can

Source: TCP

Training

Consider, again, some of the differentiating characteristics of a Kaizen company: control is shared, as are decisions, in a consensual framework, there are greater opportunities for employees to shape their jobs, there are smaller visible differences between the highest and lowest in the (flatter) hierarchy, there is an emphasis on companionship and support rather than (at best) territoriality and separation and (at worst) alienation, and there is, therefore, a tremendous emphasis on working collaboratively. The dominant management paradigm is replaced by an egalitarian paradigm; and as I said above, the leadership training that presupposes these cultural and process shifts is absolutely vital (hence the enormous effort to develop the competencies and mind sets of leaders in Kaizen companies).

But training is not just for leaders in the enablement equation: it must be (a) for all and (b) in context. Let me explain this.

Training for all

Kaizen will not work successfully if the workforce merely copies what it hears and sees by rote, or blindly follows prescriptive rules for behaviour. The whole purpose of Quality Circles/Kaizen groups is to encourage individuals to think for themselves, take the initiative, challenge received wisdom and *not* accept the status quo. Employees in a Kaizen company are not 'units of labour', they are genuinely a resource – the human resource – which is both charged with finding, and can be tapped for, ideas to improve, processes, product design and manufacturing quality.

改

Obviously, this (new) approach to their work demands an understanding of Kaizen's principles and instruments plus an ability to communicate plus multi-skill training which, by broadening the scope of everyone's work, makes the workforce a more valuable and useful resource and able to spot improvement opportunities in tasks or processes other than the ones individuals are involved with currently.

HONDA'S CORPORATE VISION STATEMENT

Honda's corporate vision statement illustrates the essence of what I have said here:

1 Quality in all jobs – *learn, think, analyze, evaluate and improve*;
2 Reliable products – on time, with excellence and consistency;
3 Better communication – listen, ask, and *speak up* (emphases added).

This is good stuff, but its implicit invitation (instruction?) to challenge received opinion intelligently and constructively is the more remarkable in the overtly hierarchical atmosphere of Japanese companies. It compares favourably to change processes in Western companies: these are invariably top-down and directed by senior management, which tends to be more concerned with expanding and protecting its authority and position than with spreading its powers. Soichiro Honda delegated all operational responsibility to concentrate his time and energies on his vision of the future for his company, something he felt sufficiently confident to do only because he had confidence in the education, training and development programmes his people had been through.

The 'challenge' flavour of Honda's vision statement is made even more explicit in the 'Ten Spartan Rules' advocated by Hideo Yoshida, founder of Dentsu, the world's largest advertising agency: 1 Create work for yourself; don't wait for it to be assigned to you; 2 Take the initiative in performing your job, instead of playing a passive part; 3 Grapple with big jobs – petty tasks debase you; 4 Choose difficult jobs. Progress lies in accomplishing difficult work; 5 Once you start a task, never give up – complete it, no matter what; 6 Lead those around you. Leading others instead of being led makes a big difference in the long run; 7 Have a plan. A long-term plan engenders perseverance, planning and effort, and gives you hope for the future; 8 Have self-confidence; otherwise your work will lack force, persistence and even substance; 9 Use your brain to the fullest degree at all times. Keep an eye on all quarters and always be on the alert. This is the way we ensure satisfactory service; 10 Don't be afraid of friction. Friction is the mother of progress and the stimulus for aggressiveness. If you fear friction, you will become servile and timid.

This is a powerful statement! and an astringent antidote to the sometimes sentimental thought that Japan's business cultures and values are based on anodyne relationships. Even in Kaizen companies, hard words can be the soul mates of hard work.

By educating and training everyone on a continuous, non-exclusive basis, the organization can achieve the goal of becoming a 'learning organization'. This is a relatively new term to Japanese business, yet one which they can readily understand as it is a natural by-product of the Kaizen way; it is occasionally misunderstood in the West, despite the

己メ

powerful writing and work of such opinion formers as Burgoyne, Pedlar and Boydell. Creating a learning organization is not the consequence of simply throwing a cornucopia of training courses at the workforce; a learning organization, as Burgoyne says, 'continuously transforms itself in the process reciprocally linked to the development of all its members; a learning organization also achieves sustainable development through enriching rather than exploiting its (market and environmental) context'. In other words, 'training' is what is done *to* people; 'learning' is what they do for themselves – and the organization does for itself – by continuously reviewing and assessing the consequences of previous actions to find ways of improving (or enhancing) positive outcomes and of eliminating anything which does not add value to the outcomes. This, then, *is* the Kaizen way of continuous improvement and continuous transformation (of products, processes and employees' competencies.)

Clearly, people who by the very nature of Kaizen are expected – required, even – to think dynamically and creatively and to be *process aware*, will not venture into such an arena and risk exposure unless they fully understand and buy into their company's culture and values and have the skills to contribute to their own and the organization's learning.

Education for all, whether it is via required attendance on provided training courses or, as is more likely in one of 'tomorrow's businesses', via monitored or self-directed experiential learning, is an essential component of building and sustaining an enabled workforce.

Training in context

Training and learning in a vacuum never make a difference in anything but the short term and to anyone but the individual. A quality of a learning organization is that its leaders regularly ask the question, What must people in our organization know next? (and employees ask the similar question, What must I learn next?) in relation to the corporate mission, objectives, strategy, tactical plans, key performance indicators and personal task competencies, and based on rigorous swot analyses conducted and acted on with such frequency that the company can maintain or improve its market position through continuous small-step transformations.

As this is the context to which I refer, and given that in a Kaizen company a significant share of the responsibility for employee education, training and development is within each team leader's and employee's personal job specification, it is now clear why Kaizen companies disseminate so much corporate and team performance information, and why leaders and employees are trained to understand and make use of it: simply, to ensure that self- and other-directed learning is indeed within context, everyone must know what this is week-by-week. Via this, the job of leadership can be delivered with a long-term perspective informed by moment-by-moment measures of performance. Process improvements and personal competency transformation can thus take place over an equally long term via localized small steps that build to produce better products and more skilled people.

Motivation

My colleague Pat Wellington wrote in her book *Kaizen Strategies for Customer Care,*

ごX

'Enough about the classic Western theories of people's needs at work and employee motivation has been written elsewhere for it not to be necessary to repeat it here. Suffice it to say that, people go to work for a variety of reasons, their expectations differ, and different aspects of work and its rewards motivate people differently. What is common and invariable, however, is each team leader's responsibility to know each employee's needs and to provide opportunities and support for them to be satisfied.

'This, though, does *not* absolve individuals from all responsibility: theirs is to take advantage of provided opportunities by participating in, for example, training and education programmes, Kaizen groups, work-team projects, suggestion systems, cross-functional collaboration and information exchange. The fact that this is so actively encouraged in Kaizen companies distinguishes them from other organizations where such a total approach to employee motivation is largely unpractised.'

I agree wholly with her sentiments. One of the greatest differences between Kaizen-inspired and more traditional Western businesses is the opportunity and encouragement for self-expression in the former. An idea, a proposal, may fall at any of the hurdles within Kaizen's consensus approach to taking action, but at least employees know that at work there will be repeated opportunities to fulfil Maslow's two pinnacle needs, satisfaction of ego (though in orthodox Kaizen companies the ego that is satisfied is the team's collective ego) and self-actualization. These are the greatest motivation drivers of people at work, and many Kaizen activities – such as those Pat has listed – offer the potential to gratify the human needs to express one's self and be acknowledged, and to exercise one's capacity to be creative.

Let me say, however, that Kaizen was never formulated

with Maslow and such psychological needs in mind; the motives were more selfish in that Kaizen's prime beneficiaries were initially and continue to be companies and, indirectly, the Japanese nation. Nonetheless, employees were overtly recognized as a valuable resource and their contributions were harnessed via Kaizen's human-centred activities. It is only with hindsight and knowledge of Maslow's classic theory after the event that Kaizen companies in Japan have recognized how powerful a motivator Kaizen's instruments and principles can be. They are beginning to take greater notice of, and to adopt, the work of our own motivation theorists to enhance the force which they have developed (albeit by chance) already. Thus, what is happening in Japanese Kaizen organizations now is what I have advocated for many years in the West – a blending of Eastern and Western philosophies and practices to create an environment which motivates teams *and* individuals at quite deep psychological levels.

Empowerment

The ultimate source of motivation is empowerment: it is *the* sign that an employer respects and trusts its employees, and is willing to let them make use of the training and development invested in them.

Let me quote from Pat Wellington's book again:

'Empowering employees is not to hand them company command and control – that, and ultimate decision-making authority, must remain with senior management . . . – but it should enable them to make and act on local decisions which influence their own work. This means that each employee and each team must be given a defined arena of functional freedom within which they can exercise their knowledge and skills. Decisions or actions which . . . take an individual or group across their arena boundary will, of course, be subject to team leader or management sanction, and this will be understood by the employees. But inside the arena the team must be free, that is empowered, to operate according to its own sanctions.'

Pat infers three interesting – almost the defining – aspects of empowerment in that paragraph:

1   The limit of any person's or team's empowerment should always be clearly delineated.

2   *Management* should be exercised at that boundary (hence the 'boundary, or hands-off, management' that I mentioned earlier), but *leadership*, especially team leadership, should be exercised within each boundary.

3   The 'sanctions' which Pat mentioned are those to which I referred: peer-owned and operated performance monitoring, appraising and disciplining.

Empowering employees, then, is:

• trusting them to make the right decisions, giving them the freedom to do so and ensuring they accept accountability

• assuring them it is all right to make mistakes as long as they learn from them and modify future behaviours accordingly

• legitimizing considered risk-taking and pushing down decision-making authority to the lowest level that risks are considered

• establishing clear lines of leadership support within each bounded arena, and managing by exception at the arena boundaries.

ASHTON PHOTO

The Ashton Photo Company is an exemplar of an empowered, team-based organization. Based since the 1930s in Salem, Oregon, the company is now in its third generation of family management. In 1993 Ashton moved into a new $3m, 44,000 square foot plant at Mill Creek. At that time, the plan was to double the $5m turnover in three years, and with volume growth of greater than 25 per cent that appears achievable.

TQM, work teams and Just-in-Time manufacturing involve every employee. Steve Ashton, the CEO, has said how strongly he believes in everyone who is influenced by a decision participating in the decision-making. All employees have a stake in the operation:

- sixteen production teams work autonomously, each is responsible directly to their customers

- employee evaluations (peer performance appraisals) follow the team concept. If an employee does not have strong support from his or her colleagues, neither a pay rise nor promotion is likely

- skill-based pay rewards employees who learn additional skills and qualify to teach them to others

- an incentive programme allocates 1 per cent of photo processing sales to be divided among hourly-paid workers each month

▶

- applicants seeking managerial posts must meet with the employees they would lead and gain their approval to secure the job

- when seasonal layoffs come, the employees with more skills – *not more seniority* – are the most likely to be retained

- if an employee is going to be affected by a company decision, he or she will first be given the opportunity to offer up questions, comments and suggestions concerning the decision (or the decision-making process)

- employees set their own working hours within their teams

- employees have absolute freedom to walk anywhere in the building (including Steve Ashton's office)

- all meetings are open, and everyone is encouraged to attend and participate

- information about budgets, sales and profits are always posted. Other information, notice and brainstorm boards allow employees to recognize good performers, float ideas and comment on the state of the company

- the 'vanilla office' – the best in the building – remains empty for everyone to use. Anyone can claim the office for their own for the day

- a 'crash room', or relaxation room, appropriately furnished, is available for any employee who feels tired, unwell or a need for privacy.

Underlying all these enablement features is the principle that no employee will get steamrollered by the management machinery.

Reward

Rewards in large Japanese companies are traditionally tied to length of service; the more years worked, the higher the salary and other rewards.

This is beginning to change in Japan as the equally potent attractors of performance-related pay, bonuses, faster promotion on personal merit, longer holidays (which it is becoming acceptable to take), and career progression through changing one's employer sweep in from the West and influence Japan's post-war system of reward. Even in Kaizen companies employees' expectations are changing as lifetime employment becomes a thing of the past and more tangible rewards (financial rewards, particularly) are being seen as a justifiable compensation for the higher personal risks that individuals are experiencing now in their careers.

This mirrors the increasingly-experienced desire to give less altruistic service to one's company and more to one's family.

What, then, is the best basis of reward for a Kaizen company in the West? As I have indicated in my narrative on Motivation, part of the fundamental nature of Kaizen is that it allows employees to express themselves, to participate, to take ownership, to respond to given responsibilities, to shape their jobs, local issues and corporate activities, and to work with different processes (via job rotation, multi-skilling, cross-functional collaboration and via partnership relationships with customers and suppliers). These are the American behavioural psychologist Herzberg's *work motivators*, and because of their critical importance to employee morale and performance I strongly advocate retaining them as foundation components of the entire reward system: the rewards themselves being the same as those I spoke of above – public praise, personal thanks, written recognition, etc; in other words, non-financial acknowledgement for work well done. Promotion within a 'league of excellent employees' falls within this form of reward.

However, employees in a Western business culture have strong expectations of financial reward too; the non-financial rewards should be supported by opportunities to earn additional remuneration determined by, for example, team performance, number of ideas contributed by the team to the suggestion system, participation in Kaizen Circles, the quality and quantity of team outputs, and so on – the base in all cases being measurable individual and team results against standards and quotas.

But, to reinforce Kaizen's focus on Herzberg's *motivators* rather than his transient *hygiene factors* (such as pay), financial rewards should never carry more 'kudos' than non-financial rewards; in other words, an employee's excellence should be measured by how many times his or her name is mentioned in the company newsletter or on notice boards and not on how much bonus has been earned. This is contrary to Western norms, where status is linked directly to pay. In the more holistic and human-centred culture of a Kaizen company, personal status is linked to the status of the team and the acknowledged quality of contributions. It is something of a rhetorical question to ask but, if you took away the pay from your people what do you provide to motivate them? If you honestly believe that your employees perceive their pay is, if you like, a 'bonus' for being where they enjoy being and doing what they enjoy doing your company is reflecting a fundamental aspect of the Kaizen philosophy.

A recent study by Dr Sharon Mason of Brock University in Ontario, Canada, showed that these are the work values aspired to by four different respondent groups:

WORK VALUES

Clerical men
1 Opportunity for advancement
2 Learn new skills
3 Wages/benefits
4 Treated with respect
5 Challenging work

Clerical women
1 Treated with respect
2 Wages/benefits
3 Learn new skills
4 Supervisor that is respected
5 Opportunity for advancement

Managerial men
1 Wages/benefits
2 Challenging work
3 Opportunity for advancement
4 Authority to make decisions
5 Sense of accomplishment

Managerial women
1 Treated with respect
2 Supervisor that is respected
3 Wages/benefits
4 Challenging work
5 Sense of accomplishment

But what about the enablement of company leaders themselves? In his book *The Rise of NEC* (Blackwell, 1991), NEC's company President, Koji Kobayashi, included his own ten-point guidelines for executives. I have reproduced them here because I applaud their simplicity as a means of self-enablement. It says much about how top business leaders in Japan can take the complex role of corporate leadership and reduce it, like a *haiku* (a descriptive poem of 17 syllables), to its essence:

1 **Make a picture of your thoughts.** Maps and sketches will provide guidance for attaining your next objective.

2 To grasp the situation in which you are now placed, **take account of a co-ordinate axis of both time and space.**

3 **Recognize that a seemingly stable corporation contains instability** while a seemingly unstable corporation can be stable.

4 **Teamwork multiplies individual abilities.** Don't forget the proverb, 'Two heads are better than one'.

5 Do not follow a one-way, single track in your thinking. **Set up feedback loops as a means of rectifying your own one-sided judgments.**

6 In any undertaking, **things develop from points to lines, and from lines to dimensions.** Keep in mind, for example, that marketing and technology form a matrix.

7 Divergence vs. convergence, the part vs. the whole – consider the advantages and disadvantages of both sides and always **cultivate a sense of balance.**

8 **Do not let yourself be swamped by the rising tide of information and knowledge.** Be selective. Remember that the most important information is not always the most obvious.

9 **Self-help is the mainstay of development** for both the individual and society.

10 **Cultivate the strong points and potentials of an individual or an enterprise and nurture them like a gardener.** It may take ten or 20 years for them to mature.

TEAM MANAGEMENT

By 'team management' I mean leadership, promoting *teamwork*, recruiting or shifting people between functions to achieve team balance and ensuring that high performance is achieved through fulfilment of nine essential and generic work functions. I will explain these in a moment, but first consider this scenario where lack of critical reasoning and teamwork were major contributory factors in a political disaster.

THE BAY OF PIGS

On 17 April 1961, US President John Kennedy gave his approval for a contingent of just under 1,500 Cuban exiles to go ashore on the swampy coast of the Bay of Pigs in Cuba and foment the revolution-by-force that would overthrow Castro and rid the United States of the communist presence in its backyard.

From that moment everything started to go wrong: the military intelligence was later shown to be weak and in vital areas wholly incorrect; none of the supply ships carrying munitions and reserves to reinforce the beachhead arrived (two were destroyed by the Cuban air force – which was supposedly incapable of mustering a single airworthy fighter – and two fled under the air assault); the swampy ground was simply too

▶

改

marshy to be traversed at speed, thus preventing all but about 200 insurgents finding cover in the jungle behind the bay; and by nightfall on the second day the exposed bulk of the invading force was surrounded by 20,000 well-armed Cuban soldiers – whom the intelligence reports had said would throw down their weapons and cross sides as soon as they heard the invasion had begun.

Castro's triumphant finalé was to claim from America $53 million ransom in food and drugs.

The failure of Kennedy's inner circle to defeat any of the false assumptions behind the invasion can at least partially be accounted for by his team's tendency to seek consensus *at the expense of sharing information, conducting a critical debate and analysis, and planning with the rigour and thoroughness the venture demanded.* In his book *Victims of Group-think** I. L. Janis hypothesized a number of reasons why the decision to invade was made. In particular, he cites what he calls the 'illusion of invulnerability' and the 'illusion of unanimity'. He wrote,

> 'When a group of people who respect each other's opinions arrives at a unanimous view each member is likely to feel that the belief *must* be true. This reliance on consensus validation tends to replace individual critical thinking and reality testing, unless there are clearcut disagreements among the members. The members of a face-to-face group often become inclined, without (consciously) realizing it (or vocalizing it), to prevent latent disagreements from surfacing, when they are about to initiate a risky course of action.' (Parentheses added.)

Other contributory factors undoubtedly played their part in the Bay of Pigs fiasco. For example, Kennedy probably did not

---

*Houghton Mifflin, 1972

know the individual strengths and weaknesses of his newly-appointed advisers, nor did he realize fully that the US Navy, Air Force and the CIA were acting independently to impress the new President with their individual prowess. In addition, there had been insufficient time to gel his new administration with the existing (cumbersome, self-serving) bureaucracy. But probably the most telling of these other contributory factors was the total disregard of lessons from the past (and America's armed forces had many to draw on from their island battles in the Pacific during the Second World War, any number of which could have been the basis of review, assessment and improvement for this particular island invasion).

I am reminded of the phrase in *Team Management** by Margerison and McCann, 'A team of brilliant individuals can often be less effective than a brilliant team of individuals.' As they say, 'It is not enough to simply assemble the best minds in the organization . . . Sound principles of team management need to be applied as well.'

Nine Key Work Functions

Margerison and McCann suggest the following nine key activities that need to be assigned to team members and managed by the team if the team is to be effective:

---

*Mercury Books, 1990 and 1995

ZX

1 *Advising* – gathering source data and information and representing it to the team as the foundation from which next actions can be planned.

2 *Innovating* – creating new ideas and thinking of new ways of improving existing processes and products.

3 *Promoting* – selling the new ideas to decision makers and identifying the resources required to turn a vision into reality.

4 *Developing* – exposing an initial concept to vigorous analysis and the concrete realities of the market today.

5 *Organizing* – utilizing the identified resources in a planned and managed structure to ensure the idea will work in the marketplace. This involves setting deadlines and establishing performance benchmarks so that progress can be monitored and measured.

6 *Producing* – fulfilling the goals.

7 *Inspecting* – ensuring that key performance indicators (quality standards, costs, production quotas, health and safety and improvements) are adhered to.

8 *Maintaining* – ensuring that the team and task infrastructures continue to support maximum efficiency. This involves maintenance of support services, personal standards, corporate values and the code of ethics that govern behaviour in the team and at work.

9 *Linking* – central to the success of all teams, as this is the leader's prime function: to co-ordinate all the team members and ensure maximum co-operation and interchange of ideas, reports, experiences and material resources.

Understanding these nine key functions, a team leader who is completely knowledgeable about his or her members' preferences, competencies, strengths and weaknesses can assign roles and responsibilities to the people best equipped to handle them. The arbitrary way in which many teams work is thus replaced by a more considered and *balanced* approach to fitting people to processes rather than whole teams to total desired results. Again, I would like to remind you of one of Kaizen's maxims: get the processes right and the right people involved in their preferred roles and the desired outcomes will follow inexorably.

Role Preferences

I am indebted to Drs Charles Margerison and Dick McCann for their seminal work on delineating team role preferences, and helping me and countless thousands of leaders in business understand how to match team responsibilities to role strengths and, importantly, *preferences for the processes integral to each role*. In *Team Management* the two authors propose eight roles that, naturally, reflect the first eight key team functions:

Creator – Innovators

These are people who innovate ideas that by their nature can challenge current thinking. Such people can be very independently minded. They need to be managed in such a way that their ideas can be stimulated and tested free of organizational constraints and such blocks to their creativity as 'we can't do that sort of thing here!' Creator – Innovators do not always fit easily into a rigidly structured environment.

Explorer – Promoters

Explorer – Promoters are usually influential, are good at making contacts, and enjoy searching for new opportunities and challenges. They are good at absorbing ideas and information and promoting projects to others.

Assessor – Developers

These people provide an essential balance between the visionaries and realists in a team. They make good analytical testers of ideas and prototypes, are enthusiastic about concepts and capable of the detailed research required to find the precise configuration which the market might want of a product.

Thruster – Organizers

Thruster – Organizers will get things done: once they are convinced that an idea is workable they will design and set up all the procedures, systems and reporting lines, organize people and material resources, and establish project mile posts and deadlines.

Concluder – Producers

Concluder – Producers enjoy producing outputs to a standard in a regular and procedural way. They do not demand the variety and dynamism that Controller – Inspectors need, to work effectively. They enjoy achieving plans and goals and the very tangibility of making a high quality product.

Controller – Inspectors

These people enjoy making sure that facts and figures are correct. They are careful, meticulous and often critical of errors and unsystematic work. Their concentration powers are enormous: they can spot variances, errors and trends in data with ease.

Upholder – Maintainers

Usually people of strong conviction, these people are often the most personally supportive of others in the team and provide a deal of stability. They are team defenders. They are consolidators, ensuring that during the 'cut and thrust' of project developments and changes team values and ethics are re-emphasized and the team remains whole and true to its beliefs.

Reporter – Advisers

The primary concern of Reporter – Advisers is to make sure that all possible information is available so that the best decisions can be made. The role of consultant or counsellor comes easily to them, as does that of facilitator. They tend not to like organizing people or projects as much as they do information.

Lee Iacocca played the part of a classic Linker. As he says in his autobiography *Iacocca – An Autobiography**,

*Bantam Books, 1986

改

'During the first couple of weeks in a new job, you look for tell-tale signs. You want to know what kind of fraternity you have joined.'

He went on to say of his early days at the Chrysler Motor Corporation,

'Everyone worked independently . . . All of Chrysler's problems really boiled down to the same thing. Nobody knew who was on first. There was no team, only a collection of independent players, many of whom hadn't yet mastered their positions.'

Iacocca reformed all Chrysler's work teams, balancing them to ensure intra-team efficiency, with himself at the centre as the orchestrator or principal Linker.

In this position, responsible for redefining culture, values, order of conduct, relationships, roles and corporate goals, Iacocca exercised the team management skills of an effective team leader:

- active listening
- communicating
- problem-solving
- counselling
- team developing
- work allocating
- team relating
- delegating
- setting quality standards
- setting objectives
- interface managing

- participative decision-making
- results monitoring
- costs controlling.

SUMMARY

On 24 October 1910 US President Theodore Roosevelt said in a speech he delivered to businessmen in New York,

> 'People ask the difference between a leader and a boss . . . The leader works in the open, and the boss in covert.'

Nearly 70 years later Prince Charles said in a speech that he gave to the Parliamentary and Scientific Committee,

> 'British management doesn't seem to understand the importance of the human factor.'

This chapter has underscored the importance that Kaizen leaders place on being personally visible and working with a fully understood human resource.

They emphasize the allure of enabling individuals and teams through communication, training, motivation, empowerment and reward. They are good team managers – or Linkers – and promote teamwork by assigning roles and responsibilities according to the role strengths and weaknesses of their team members, to fulfil the nine key team functions.

They are people-centred, and recognize that nothing will be achieved without the willing collaboration of employees. In this, their *goal* is the results expected of their team by the company; their *focus* is the team; and the *means* by which they achieve the goal is the process of leadership.

VACUUM MOULD INDUSTRY, TOKYO

Vacuum Mould Industry Ltd is one of Japan's many medium-sized companies. Founded in the 1960s by its current President, Takashi Kitazawa, it employs 130 people making vacuum moulded products which are used as, for example, disposable food packaging and car dashboards. The company was one of the first to introduce vacuum moulding technology to Japan and, compared with other companies in the sector, has a record of success in growth and profitability.

One of the keys to the company's success, according to its President, is an extremely unusual factor: his own blindness. When he was 33, at a time when the company had grown to 40 employees, Mr Kitazawa suddenly lost his sight. With help from his wife and other employees, he decided to continue running the company and evolved a new and effective style of leadership accommodating his blindness. For instance, he:

- stepped back from daily involvement in production work to consider the larger issues: How should the company develop? What new equipment or technologies should be purchased? How can the employees be more motivated and satisfied?

- analyzed the details of production, organization and co-ordination; as he could not see the manufacturing process or technical drawings, other people had to describe shapes and processes to him. The detailed questions he had to ask to understand fully what was happening often led to ideas for improvements.

In retrospect, Mr Kitazawa thinks that these new roles – which were forced on him – were major reasons for the company's success. He feels that too often in small and medium-sized companies, the managing director is so involved in daily problems that he or she can neither see the broader picture nor focus in sufficient detail on specific problem areas.

The major problem for him now is to find and train other people to think and work like himself, first to share his role now the company is larger, and later to be able to take over from him.

He feels it is vital that people in charge of small and medium-sized companies treat their role as leaders more seriously. Like the leaders of larger enterprises they should concentrate on 'seeing' the major issues for their organization, rather than on 'doing' things which other people in the company can do. Only in this way, he believes, will companies have the vision to succeed.

To answer the question in the chapter title, 'What will be the role of tomorrow's leaders?' my answer is in two parts: first, a team leader's role will be to achieve team balance and first-class linking, thereby creating a high-performance team. This sounds simple, but maintaining team balance in an environment of market and demand turbulence calls for an extraordinarily high understanding of human dynamics plus a highly-tuned ability to motivate and stretch individual performance whilst keeping intact the team's 'zone of psychological security and integrity'. To put it crudely, the leader must be able to take the flak and maintain team discipline and

改

solidity. Linking skills thus have an importance of the first magnitude.

Second, the individual and collective roles of top and central management will be to:

- structure – and restructure – the business
- identify and appoint to senior management positions those who have demonstrated on merit the potential to handle increased responsibility and accountability
- approve (or reject) requests for capital investments
- approve (or request reconsideration of) sub-units' business plans
- monitor the performance of these sub-units
- acquire (or divest) business
- steer the globalization of their business (including the globalization of marketing, advertising, PR, product design and product distribution)
- make (or sever) strategic alliances and channel partnerships
- raise and dispose of financial resources
- represent the business to internal and external stakeholders
- develop and constantly refine a clear and coherent corporate vision, and ensure total corporate integration and alignment.

NEC

In his book *The Rise of NEC** Koji Kobayashi, the company's President, wrote in a section entitled 'Toward Dynamism and Flexibility: The Primacy of People',

> 'My organizational philosophy is very different from the bureaucratic views that prevail in government agencies . . . People come first . . . the first step is assigning a person to the job: and drawing up an organizational chart is only possible when all the personnel assignments have been made.'

As he says, he called upon 'everyone in the company to be "more dynamic and more flexible", concentrating in those two terms all my aspirations for the company – *an end to rigidity, freedom from fixed ideas, better communications between area and function levels, and greater individual initiative.*'

In January 1972 Kobayashi announced to the entire company that from then on the guiding principle behind all business conducted at or by NEC would be quality, but not just product quality. It is interesting to note that of the seven points in his Operation Quality campaign, only one concerns product and services; the rest are concerned with human-centred factors:

1 Improve the quality of management.
2 Improve the quality of products and services.
3 Improve the quality of the working environment.
4 Improve the quality of working relations.
5 Improve the quality of human behaviour.
6 Improve the quality of business performance (through improved co-operation).
7 Improve the quality of corporate image.

He writes, 'Having proposed here seven Qs, I called on all the employees to set their own goals and promote their own projects based upon them.'

---

*Blackwell, 1991

乙犬

Like Sir Graham Day, ex-Chairman of Powergen plc, I am drawn to the words of Professor Abraham Zaleznik (a tutor at Harvard's Graduate School of Business): '**Leadership is made of substance, humanity and morality . . .**' In an item Sir Graham contributed to *The Lust for Leadership** he wrote:

'Leadership is the ability to change compelled performers into willing participants. If you only have a mandatory leadership, you have the three negatives: pressure without motivation; process without substance; organization without improvement. True leadership addresses those negatives. The attributes which ultimately matter most are the abilities to communicate and inspire.'

This sentiment encapsulates the Europe Japan Centre's view – and my presentations on leadership – exactly.

---

*Simon Caulkin, Management Today, November 1993

3

WHO WILL BE TOMORROW'S LEADERS?

改善

INTRODUCTION

That is an interesting question, to which there are a number of answers any of which could be right. Or wrong. It depends on whose view of tomorrow you subscribe to. Given that the picture of the future is changing rapidly, I might argue that the only sensible answer is that suggested by Darwin – those who will be leaders are those who through adaptation become the most fitted for the job.

To be more pragmatic, it is a question I have debated with leaders internationally and, although few arrive at exactly the same interpretation of the signs, most agree on three points: first, a colossal paradigm shift from current practices is inevitable; second, the human resource is central to survival, and development investment in it will become increasingly important during the next two years; and third, there is no 'single malt' model that at this time represents an ideal model for the next millennium. Rather, they say, a blend of American, European and Japanese practices is likely to prove the most robust and palatable 'beverage'.

However, while such a marriage between the best from the East and West undoubtedly brings with it many blessings, the capricious children of the 1980s and 1990s – redundancies and the new technologies – have somehow to be accommodated humanely within the union. Such factors, then, as the qualities which comprise the current base lines from which today's companies prepare for their futures, the degree of optimism that colours today's leaders' perspectives, corporate flexibility, and how perfectly organizations adapt their workforces – and employees adapt themselves – will determine who leads tomorrow's businesses internally and externally.

Let me now put some flesh on these introductory remarks, drawn from the opinions of a number of business leaders. First, I will précis the somewhat pessimistic views of Jeremy Rifkin, President of the Foundation on Economic Trends in Washington, DC. Second, I will discuss the cautiously optimistic strategies adopted by Nynex and Matsushita and finally, I will present the successful practices of Dettmers Industries.

THE END OF WORK – THE END OF LEADERS?

The End of Work is the title of Jeremy Rifkin's latest book. In it he depicts the rise and consequences of automation and the information revolution from, what I consider to be, the standpoint of a very worst case scenario. The thrust of his arguments makes riveting if not nightmarish reading, yet I suspect the rest of us would be unwise to dismiss his thesis entirely out of hand as self-serving sensationalism.

The core message in *The End of Work* is this: In the 1960s 33 per cent of all workers were in blue-collar employment; today in America it is down to 17 per cent, yet the United

States is still out-producing the rest of the world. Rifkin contends that, by the year 2025 only 2 per cent of the world's workforce will be in blue-collar factory work. This dramatic decline in the need for skilled and semi-skilled producers, once the backbone of every company, is due, he says, to automation and the maturing of the Information Age. In an interview published in *Newsweek** Rifkin said,

> 'The hope was (that) the service area would absorb blue-collar jobs, but now the technological revolution is invading the services. We have virtual companies, flattened to a small *entrepreneurial leadership*, a technical staff and a core staff . . . Wholesalers are being eliminated as manufacturers deal with retailers directly through electronic interchange. White-collar middle management, secretaries, receptionists are going. The trickle-down technology argument is not true today. Even if someone came up with a new product that had universal market potential, you could build (it) in workerless factories and market it with virtual companies. What that will mean is the inevitable decline of mass labour.'

If this view of a technological Utopia is to be believed, the implications for leadership – its qualities, competencies and implementation – are huge. Who, for example, will leaders lead? What sectors will still employ staff and, thus, still need leaders? Will individuals become single operators leading no-one but themselves?

Rifkin says that the only new sector (the one that will rise to the pinnacle of business) is what he calls the 'Knowledge Sector', comprising 'symbolic analysts, engineers, scientists,

*24 April 1995

ZX

computer programmers, entertainers, accountants and lawyers'. But so limited will be the number employed in these functions that there will never be sufficient openings to absorb the countless millions who will be sliced out of manufacturing, the service industries and agriculture.

What this boils down to is, as Rifkin says in his book, the kiss of death: as wholesale redundancies rob people of their prime source of revenue, the wealth to purchase the increased productivity made possible by automation (which, of course, triggered the redundancies) will evaporate simultaneously. He calls this the Achilles' heel of the Information Age: short-term savings made by replacing staff with robotics, but long-term decline due to a loss of purchasing power in the marketplace.

But what of the upsides, the positive consequences of the technology revolution? Needless to say, there are and will continue to be many, from 24-hour electronic personal banking to key-hole surgery and truly individually-customized product manufacture where, for example, a customer can commission the Levi Company to make a pair of jeans tailored to their personal specifications using the same computer controlled mass production techniques used by the company for its own standard products. The same is beginning to happen in the motor industry; customers want the technical reliability and build quality of automated production, but they also want an individual car, rather than a standard 'Euromobile', reflecting personal tastes. Rifkin sees the benefits of the Information Age triggering a renaissance for human civilization, though I see his future as something like the curate's egg: good only in parts. He says that we will be freer to pursue more leisure activities and to engage in service and advocacy jobs in non-profit community, civic, spiritual and family-related work. As Rifkin said in the *Newsweek* interview, 'Social skills are the only ones . . . computer(s) can't take over.' That for me is the good part; it must be balanced by the fundamental psychological need to perform meaningful work, each of us doing what we are inherently or intuitively capable and desirous of doing and receiving tangible rewards that have real utility and exchange value. The bad part of the egg in Rifkin's future is that the opportunities for fulfilling personal potential are few except for those who are in (or, by retraining, move into) the Knowledge Sector, and are willing to reduce their working week to 30 hours so that the total available working hours can be shared more equitably than they are at present (where some employees work overtime and others do not work at all.) Rifkin's final comment is chilling, even though we have heard it before and know it to be true despite politicians of all colours arguing that unemployment has only minimal influence on the disintegration of social values: 'People forced out of the marketplace will take by force what they can't earn.'

Rifkin's *The End of Work* is a potent book; his arguments are cogent and presented with a fascinating and mesmeric logicality, yet is his future the only future for today's companies, employees and leaders? Are we on the threshold of the world of *Blade Runner* or can we use all our skills to avert a workforce disaster of epic proportions?

There is no doubt that Information Technology ('Informating', as current jargon puts it) is changing radically the way businesses are organized and the way people work. Instantaneous knowledge exchange creates greater transparency and new ideas about how tasks can be processed.

CHIAT DAY INC.

Jay Chiat, Managing Partner at Chiat Day Inc. in New York has reformed his company around the 'virtual office', a physical office but into which employees come and go around the clock as they please and in which there is now more electronic communication than face-to-face interaction. He sees IT as personally empowering and liberating. His staff operate as outworkers: as he said, it's not *where* employees work that matters it's *what* they're doing. He, also liberated from many of a manager's classic people-management functions, has had to let go and come to trust his largely unseen workers that they will fulfil their responsibilities, but as he moved away from close-quarters supervision to boundary management – where he monitors task results – he created Chiat Day's open arena in which his project-centred employees now manage their own work processes.

IDEO PRODUCT DEVELOPMENT

Tom Kelly, Marketing Manager at Ideo Product Development in California, has taken the virtual office and Tom Peters' project-based working one step on: like Chiat Day, Ideo is also located in a physical building, but their offices are seen as 'spaces' rather than rooms of fixed dimension with set positions for the office furniture; all the furniture – partitions, desks, filing cabinets, book cases – are on wheels which means that at a moment's notice a space can be reconfigured to suit the particular needs of a project team. He calls this 'moving your nest around the tree'. Kelly, however, recognizes that person-to-person interaction at arm's length, via e-mail, voice mail or *virtuality* (computerland) cuts across a basic human need to interact face-to-face and he has therefore initiated Monday morning get-togethers to discuss not business but, specifically and exclusively, what people did over the weekend.

Both Chiat and Kelly have found that IT has enhanced task flexibility, enabled team-controlled project working and freed employees to design and manage their own work processes. As George Fisher, Chairman, President and Chief Executive Officer of Eastman Kodak at Rochester, New York, has remarked, leaders must achieve the balance between employees as human beings and employees working like automatons at keyboards. He sees the new technologies as 'enablers', enabling his people to spend more time with customers and colleagues.

Today's leaders have the capacity – and increasingly the need – to ensure that lean-and-mean companies are not hollow. Two other companies, amongst thousands around the world, have decided that, while technological advances cannot be uninvented or reversed they will still invest in their human resource, though its form, function and tenure will change.

Tomorrow's *internal* leaders will emerge from what these companies are doing.

NYNEX AND MATSUSHITA

Nynex is New York's local telephone company. It is a typical US organization in that its employees enjoy many opportunities to shine, to earn merit bonuses and to advance their careers rapidly (sometimes meteorically); until recently, however, they also never knew when they might lose their job due either to frequent departmental or corporate restructuring or the idiosyncrasies of a manager.

▶

Matsushita Electric is a giant global trader presided over by Yoichi Morishita. It is a Kaizen company, and employees working for Matsushita used to enjoy a job for life; they continue to benefit from the supportive and communicative environment of a team-based culture and steady though unremarkable career progress for some. There are considerably fewer opportunities to earn personal merit rewards than in Nynex.

Both companies face the same future, and must consider the same contributory factors, as that looked at by Jeremy Rifkin. To begin with Robert Thrasher, vice president for re-engineering at Nynex, and Morishita considered the options open to their companies, then took the paths an observer could well have expected them to take: Thrasher to slice out 35,000 jobs by 1996 as a quick and expedient way of streamlining an over-manned business, and Morishita to protect every one of his 90,000 'salarymen', despite the economic pressures, in a show of paternalistic loyalty.

Had these companies continued to follow these paths neither would have merited attention other than in local newspapers and in-house journals. As it is, Nynex has adopted some practices from the East and Matsushita has adopted some from the West, in the former case to minimize the 'mean' in Thrasher's rebuilding of a lean-and-mean telecoms operation, and in the latter to stimulate more adventurous personal performance, and opportunities at the top for those coming in at the bottom thus progressing their careers with more gusto.

In neither case has it been a simple instance of switching strategic tack; Thrasher is a hard, outspoken, task-focused Controller, comfortable with achieving goals irrespective of people's feelings and ruffled feathers; Morishita is as self-effacing and quiet as Thrasher is demonstrative, fiercely protective of his workforce and he honours the code of non-confrontation, of not losing face (either his own or anyone else's), of listening intently to argument and counter-argument and then either taking a long-considered decision or delegating it to a team for a consensus decision but always invoking Konosuke Matsushita's expectation of mutual loyalty. Both men – supreme leaders in their own cultures – have had to change *personal* tack and adapt their handling of the same set of environmental forces, to accommodate technological advances, changes in trading conditions and human needs, by blending two very different business cultures to create a powerful – and more humane – approach to the task of restructuring. A 'single malt' model would have ensured short-term survival, particularly in Nynex's case, but in neither would it have left the company prepared for long-term growth.

In the Spring of 1994 Thrasher approved an entirely new way of handling the situation at Nynex, that US Secretary of Labor, Robert Reich, called 'a breakthrough in American labour relations'. The renegotiated contracts require Nynex's employees to work harder, perform more tasks and be more job flexible; they include large pensions for early retirees, and free education and retraining at college. But the important point is that forced redundancies have been virtually debarred through to the end of 1998. It will cost Nynex over $3 billion in restructuring charges well into 1996 to lay-off surplus employees more gently. And those that do leave will be better prepared with the company's help to take advantage of their new personal futures.

Morishita, too, is a proponent of *risutora*, or restructuring, and he is, as I indicated, introducing Western practices to achieve his corporate aims. For example, he is reducing Matsushita's workforce through natural wastage and not replacing employees who leave with recruits. (This *is* a noteworthy devel-

▶

opment for an organization like Matsushita which until 1994, in the company of many other Japanese employers, recruited really quite large numbers of school and university leavers under instruction from the government to keep the national unemployment rate low – as it has officially been (below 3 per cent) for decades. In addition, Morishita replaced the time-honoured system of management and executive bonus payments based on length-of-service seniority with one based on quality of performance. For the first time the company is now hiring scientists, researchers and some functional heads on a contract basis rather than as permanent employees on the established staff. The upshot of all this is virtually the same as we have seen in Nynex: employees who are being stretched without direct extra reward and, as you might expect in a Kaizen organization, great investment in education and training/retraining to, as Morishita says, 'teach salarymen to think like managers'.

Michael Hirst wrote in *Newsweek**,

'The transformation of unflinching bottom-liners [Thrasher] into touchy-feely advocates of human relations, and of paternalists [Matsushita] into martinets, is part of a large-scale rethinking in the advanced economies over what to do about jobs: how to eliminate redundant ones, how to create new ones. It is also about how companies can get and keep skilled workers at a time when streamlined operations and tougher competition demand more of employees than ever.'

*6 February 1995

Clearly, the behaviour of leaders can have a tremendous impact on this squaring of the circle, not least in terms of maintaining company (and personal) loyalty and commitment from those who are left following organizational restructuring. So-called 'slash and burn' experts, or hatchet-men, are useful for only one thing, which disqualifies them from corporate leadership: you end up with a company of mercenaries, as Peter Scott-Morgan, a frequently-quoted trans-Atlantic consultant, has said, and that can make leanness and loyalty mutually contradictory. Similarly, undiluted philanthropy is an uncomfortable bedfellow of hard-edged realism and commercial pragmatism.

If this has crudely described the typical Western and Eastern approaches to organizational development in the early 1990s then the distinction is blurring under the influence of cross-pollinated ideas from different business philosophies. American, Japanese and European leadership styles at large still remain distinct, but convergence is accelerating. Michael Hammer's book *Reengineering the Corporation*, for instance, sold 250,000 copies in Japan alone. Leaders who look beyond their own borders and utilize the best of what other cultures offer are those who will be with us tomorrow.

WHO WILL BE TOMORROW'S 'CULTURAL' LEADERS?

'Stakeholder power', by which I mean the influence on a company exerted by customers, shareholders, financial institutions and sometimes local communities, is a force that can underpin or undermine corporate survival – and, indeed, the ζズ

survival of individual leaders. Customers and shareholders of, for example, the privatized utility companies in the UK are only now beginning to understand the potency of their influence and to exercise it, as a consequence of the perceived unfairness and inequalities of the treatment meted out to staff and chief executives, the salaries earned by those at the top and those on the shopfloor, and the costs to customers of gas, electricity, water and telephone calls. Although the chief executives of British Gas and a number of the Regional water companies were 'protected' in recent votes of confidence by institutional shareholders, individual shareholders created enough waves to compel the government to review utility prices and initiate the Greenbury Committee's investigation into top people's salaries. The whole issue, including the 'protectionist stand' taken by the institutions, has been on the open agenda at the House of Commons for nearly 15 months (up to July 1995); it will likely not be resolved until personal investors believe that their voice is being heard as loudly as that of pension fund trustees (the biggest shareholders in the UK), politicians and some companies quoted on the Stock Exchange. Their belief might well be groundless and supported by little else than what has been reported in the Western media of the Japanese financial capital system and a presumption that the same applies here.

Since the end of the Second World War, when co-operation between Japan's government, banks, industry and workers was essential to ensure recovery, strong links between politicians, civil servants, finance and industry have given Japan huge advantages. Japanese companies have been able to afford long-term relationships with their employees because Japanese investors, protected by the mutually-supportive economic–political–trading complex, have long-term relationships with them. Companies like Matsushita have been shielded from market fluctuations and promiscuous individual investors by cross-shareholding relationships with banks and often long-term stakeholders. At the same time in America and the UK (but less so in Germany) short-termism has meant a tremendous pressure on companies to return quick profits that satisfy banks, institutional fund-holders and capricious personal shareholders.

However, as human resource strategies and practices are beginning to converge so too are the structures of capital that underpin the economies in the US and Japan. The American market, for example, now encourages and rewards good labour relations and personnel policies that build rather than destroy workforce competencies and skills pools; and banks can now own stock in companies allowing them to build Japanese-style long-term relationships. Japanese companies, on the other hand, are increasingly needing to show short-term dividends to satisfy investors influenced by international standards. This will inevitably add pace to the speed with which such human resource practices as lifetime employment and open-door recruitment are changed.

Clearly, then, two broad movements are changing the world of work: one is the convergence of the economic structures which support the world's three great trading powerhouses, America, Japan and Europe; the other, also the subject of convergence of practices, is the high profile that people – employees and shareholders – are now enjoying. We can see how those companies which temper a headlong rush for technology with human-centred employee development will first, produce tomorrow's leaders and second, attract the

改

investment needed to carry them on to the next millennium. So far, a lot of this is happening at the margins, but when such globally-influential Kaizen companies like Matsushita and smaller though no less locally-influential Kaizen companies like Nynex attract attention because significant changes have happened organizationally and attitudinally, we can be sure that leadership itself is crossing the line separating the 'me' generation of the 1980s and the 'you also' generation of the knowledge-based late 1990s.

WHAT DOES IT ALL MEAN TO LEADERS?

To lead effectively, future leaders at *all* levels will have to become:

- strategic opportunists
- globally aware
- capable of managing highly-decentralized organizations.

This view, with which we at the Europe Japan Centre whole-heartedly concur, is J. A. Conger's. Writing in 'The Brave New World of Leadership Training' in *Organisational Dynamics** and in 'Training Leaders for the Twenty-First Century',† Conger of McGill University added,

> '. . . the workforce (of the future) will not only be more diverse (consisting of more women and minority groups whose cultures, education, grasp of basic English and maths will be different

---

*American Management Association, New York; Winter, 1993
†*Human Resource Management Review*, JAI Press Inc.; Volume 3 Number 3, 1993

from that today) but also one that is less tolerant of the interpersonal weaknesses of their superiors. With the increasing emphasis on organizational behaviour in management schools, the appearance of employee rights Acts, and a greater public awareness of "effective" interpersonal behaviour . . . subordinates will expect their leaders to be more interpersonally competent. Those who are not will face a host of barriers to being truly influential as organizational leaders.

'The shift, however, is only a manifestation of something more profound and fundamental – the increasing importance of the workplace as a person's primary community in life.'

Conger proposes that tomorrow's leaders will require six competencies, three which are defined by and will help the leader operate in the marketplace, and three defined by and which will help the leader relate to and manage the workforce:

- strategic leadership
- global leadership } marketplace dependent
- post-hierarchical leadership

- diversity leadership
- interpersonal leadership } workforce dependent
- community leadership

In *Organizing for the Future** M. W. McCall included the following in the article 'Developing Leadership':

'Not everyone is cut out to be a leader, much less a leader in the turbulent corporate environment of the years ahead. Not everyone is cut out to be a great pianist or an Olympic runner either,

---

*Edited by J. R. Galbraith and E. E. Lawler; Josey Bass, California, 1993

改

but there is a significant lesson in the difference. When great talents are found in these spheres, they are trained and nurtured. To be sure, they enter challenging competitions relative to their current level of development, but each such trial is viewed as a learning event, to be critiqued and learned from. Typical corporate practice stands in stark contrast: take promising talent, throw it into tough assignments, stand back, and watch what happens. Survivors, it is assumed, must have "the right stuff" or must have learned by virtue of having the experience. But no great pianist or runner, no matter how naturally gifted, has achieved greatness without years of practice, learning, dedication, and sacrifice. Similar hard work is at the core of developing leadership attributes. *It is not survival of the fittest that counts; it is development of the fittest.* Organizations, then, face two substantial challenges if they hope to have effective leaders: they must identify those who have the potential to acquire the (competencies), and they must nurture them as tenaciously and carefully as they would nurture any other . . . resource critical to success.'

In a nutshell, and reflecting the themes I explored in chapter 2, I suggest that tomorrow's leaders will be those who are developed to:

- ask questions and listen to all answers
- solve problems by drawing on in-team solutions and solutions implemented elsewhere
- train, coach, educate and counsel their team in job and team interaction skills
- facilitate team interaction by balancing roles and responsibilities and diversity
- manage team boundaries, by personally letting go and encouraging team self-directedness

- co-ordinate cross-functional collaboration
- provide formal and informal recognition and reward
- stretch themselves and their teams to the limit
- analyze competitors, and industry trends and prepare appropriate strategic and tactical responses
- consider human values as well as financial or performance targets
- inspire loyalty and create enjoyment in what people do
- inform
- create a constant pursuit of purpose for continual improvement of products and service
- provide employees with opportunities to develop their full potential
- channel employees' efforts towards the achievement of heroic goals
- deliver empowerment and encourage creative, dynamic thinking
- create a knowledge-based culture
- understanding the relationship between home and work
- trust.

DETTMERS INDUSTRIES

I must thank Michael Dettmers, with whom I have shared many conference platforms, for the following summary of why *Inc.* magazine voted Dettmers Industries one of the 'Best Small Companies to Work for in America'.

'CREATING FLEXIBILITY AND INSTILLING ENTREPRENEURSHIP'

Introduction

The globalization of the marketplace has brought challenges that few business leaders anticipated. Technological innovation, global competition, environmental pollution, market fragmentation and information overload are altering the way we live and do business. Globalization has also transformed labour into a worldwide commodity. As a consequence, many workers are experiencing a general decline in their standard of living, a condition which is producing increased cynicism and frustration.

In a rapidly changing world, business practices must be continually reinvented. And they must be designed with the intention of shifting this mood of cynicism and frustration to one of hope and ambition. In short, business leaders must invest ways to infuse a spirit of entrepreneurship throughout their organizations.

The 21st Century Enterprise

Dettmers Industries is committed to meeting this challenge. Our experience in manufacturing seating and table products for the corporate aviation industry has convinced us that competition in the 21st Century will be dominated by agile enterprises. For the better part of the 20th Century, businesses valued efficiency and economies of scale which were achieved through centralized corporate policies and financial controls in hierarchical structures.

The agile enterprise, on the other hand, values creativity and flexibility. It emphasizes teamwork over individualism, seeks global over domestic markets, and focuses on customers, not short-term profits. In this way, it is able to bring out totally new products and services quickly. It assimilates field experience and technological innovation, continually modifying and improving its products and services.

Agile enterprises produce to order rather than to stock and sell. They measure quality by assessing customer satisfaction during the full life of the product. Agile enterprises continuously invest in the skill base of their employees because they are valued as the company's prime resource. The workforce is responsible for innovation, product and service evolution and for production process improvements. Agility is accomplished by integrating technology, management and the workforce into a co-ordinated, interdependent system. The agile enterprise is the next natural development in business. Those companies that focus now on transitioning to agile production systems will become the strongest competitors in the global marketplace.

Agile manufacturing at Dettmers Industries

At Dettmers Industries, our workforce is organized into *multi-disciplinary* product teams which are responsible for the total manufacturing process.

Teams elect their leaders, hire their own personnel, set their own schedules and are responsible for product as well as process improvements. In doing so, teamwork, dignity, and pride of ownership are fostered throughout the workplace.

▶

> Compensation is team-based, each team receiving a fixed percentage of the sale price of the products it manufactures. The more productive a team is, the more money each of its members earns. Thus, we are able to shift the 'wage–labour' paradigm* by providing an opportunity for our employees to

*PARADIGMS

It was Thomas Kuhn in his book *The Structure of Scientific Revolutions* (University of Chicago Press, 1962) who coined the term 'paradigms' to describe mental models. He defined a paradigm as: **'a constellation of concepts, values, perceptions and practices shared by a community which forms a particular vision of reality that is the basis of the way a community organizes itself'**. It is important to note the implication in 'paradigm' of the *shared* nature of the belief system: an individual can hold a 'mindset' (a term I myself used earlier when describing the constituents of a Kaizen leader's mindset), but a 'paradigm' is always shared by a community. Thus, Dettmers Industries' old wage-labour paradigm – in which the *whole* workforce believed in the sterile work–pay–work cycle – was changed to an entirely new system, a new paradigm again believed in by everyone.

As Richard Pascale wrote in his book *Managing on the Edge†*,

> 'Our [Western managements'] problem lies with assumptions so deeply internalized that they are truly "within us". That's why our efforts to emulate the Japanese seldom close the competitive gap. That's why . . . nothing short of a shift in our thinking, discontinuous with the past, is necessary . . . This is not to suggest that the Japanese have the new paradigm all locked up, but that our evolving paradigm needs to embrace a set of ideas that theirs has already encompassed.'

†Simon and Schuster, 1990

plan and work towards fulfilling financial goals they set for themselves and their families. By designing and implementing a system which infuses the entrepreneurial spirit throughout our organization, we have increased productivity, quality, innovation, reduced cycle times, and reversed the trend towards ever lower standards of living.

Training at Dettmers Industries

To help our employees optimize their potential under this system, we have developed a comprehensive training programme which teaches skills for effective teamwork, communication, learning, innovation and customer satisfaction. Our programme comprises workshops, seminars and courses, many of which are accredited by Indian River Community College in Stuart, Florida. Each course is a dynamic learning experience achieved by incorporating a mix of dialogue, group discussions, lectures, exercises, simulations, readings and written assignments.

Our programme recognizes the importance of teaching skills which allow different people to trust, to make agreements and to invent possibilities together, regardless of their differences. Unfortunately, our educational system is designed to transfer knowledge and skills to individuals. It is ill-equipped to train people to learn and work in the team-based flexible organizations of the future. To compensate for this deficiency, businesses themselves must provide this training if they intend to compete in the emerging global economy.

It is important to emphasize that we redesigned our organization before we implemented our training programme. Only after we invented a game which was capable of infusing the entrepreneurial spirit throughout our organization were we in a position to design a training programme to complement it. This

▶

is important because for training to be effective, it must be perceived as a benefit to the recipients. When we provide training in teamwork, for example, our employees perceive it as benefiting themselves because our system rewards teams for their productivity. Without organizational redesign, however, training in teamwork is often perceived by employees as benefiting management and shareholders and is usually less effective.

Principles upon which our programme is based

During the transition to agile manufacturing at Dettmers Industries, drawing upon the ground-breaking work of Dr Fernandez Flores, we identified four new paradigm business principles which form the cornerstones of our training programme. They are:

- universal pragmatics of action
- organizing for innovation
- business process design
- creating a learning organization.

We refer to these principles as 'new paradigm' because they are a reinterpretation of conventional wisdom and common sense about business and management. A new paradigm opens two kinds of opportunities. First, the opportunity to address current breakdowns by designing more effective practices. Second, the opportunity to bring forth entirely new possibilities that could not be envisioned within the framework of the old interpretation.

Old paradigm organizations are characterized by autocratic management styles well-suited to hierarchical structures. This style is dysfunctional in new paradigm organizations where work is performed by teams not individuals, where hierarchy is superseded by networks, where expectations are driven by personal growth not just security, where the workforce is culturally diverse not homogeneous, and where knowledge and information are more significant resources than capital. New paradigm organizations require people who are flexible and capable of co-ordinating action effectively in the midst of permanent change and uncertainty. In short, agility is the new paradigm in business.

Universal pragmatics of action

Improving co-ordination between people is becoming a central issue in business today. Business must integrate the activities of teams and individuals, sometimes on a global scale. Furthermore, this co-ordination must be fast and flexible, capable of adjusting to rapidly changing market conditions. A system called 'universal pragmatics of action' brings elegant simplicity to this complex and challenging task. It involves viewing co-ordination as a simple conversation or 'workflow'. This conversation consists of a few basic moves in language called speech acts. In making a speech act, a person is taking a commitment about how he or she and those listening will co-ordinate action in the future.

Human beings live in language, but few appreciate the power of language to create the future. Most people understand language as a vehicle for describing reality, transmitting information and expressing ideas and feelings. The new paradigm in business shifts the focus from this descriptive or passive interpretation to a 'generative' interpretation of language. The generative capabilities of language – requests, promises, offers and declarations – enable people to co-ordinate action more effectively. When these skills are mastered, it is easier to design organizations as networks of commitments. The result is less hierarchy, increased flexibility, better teamwork, and improved productivity.

▶

▶

Organizing for innovation

Conventional wisdom holds that innovation is a mysterious process, associated with artistic creativity. This concept has led to
the 'Silicon Valley' approach to innovation: put a few bright
people in a room, add money and resources, and hope for the
best. Innovation is so important in today's global marketplace
that this approach is no longer adequate. In the new paradigm,
innovation is not viewed as a rare and mysterious process,
reserved for a few exceptionally talented people. If the correct
organizational conditions are present, the capacity for innovation can be taught and widely practised. Innovation can be
divided into three major categories:

● continuous innovation

● improving core technologies

● radical innovation.

Continuous innovation involves improving products or services
incrementally. By improving core technologies, new products
and services can be created. The fax machine is an example of
a product that depends on several core technologies (tele-
phony, photocopying, microelectronics). Radical innovation
produces dramatic breakthroughs that make whole new markets or ways of doing things possible. Examples include peni-
cillin, aeroplanes, computers, and television. Learning
organizations are led by people who create and maintain the
structure and conditions necessary to foster innovation in all
three categories.

Business process design

Business process design seeks dramatic improvements in productivity by zeroing-in on processes that are central to any
business. Core processes common to most organizations
include product development, customer service, and order
fulfilment. Process design produces a framework for mapping

and analyzing the features of a particular business process. In doing so, it integrates concerns for quality, cycle time, innovation and customer satisfaction. By observing and specifying recurrent flows of work in organizations, it is possible to establish systematic programmes of continuous improvement.

One strategy for cutting costs and compressing a core business process involves empowering the staff closest to the customer with the authority and tools to make more decisions. The goal is to let one person perform the work of many. Another strategy is to create cross-functional teams of employees who work concurrently and are in regular contact so each is aware of changes that may affect his or her job. This approach is particularly effective in product development. Technology is a support structure that automates business processes involving information. E-mail is useful for *ad hoc* processes such as product development, where one step affects another. Workflow software excels at automating more structured processes such as order fulfilment where the same steps are repeated.

Once practitioners are trained in this system, they are able to anticipate problems and opportunities, and design new structures to address them. When these critical processes are well designed, costs and cycle times throughout the organization are reduced. Processes such as contract and project management are also more easily accomplished. Creating agreements among participants to effectively co-ordinate action lies at the heart of business process design.

Creating a learning organization

Management theorists such as Peter Drucker, Peter Senge and David Garvin have focused our attention on the 'learning organization'. According to Garvin, a learning organization is skilled at creating, acquiring, and transferring knowledge, and at modifying behaviour to reflect new knowledge and insights. Learning organizations exhibit skills in five main categories:

- systematic problem solving
- experimenting with new approaches
- learning from past experience
- learning from the experiences of others
- transferring knowledge quickly throughout the organization.

While many companies practise these activities to some degree, few are consistently successful because they rely largely on happenstance and isolated examples. By creating systems and processes that support these activities, and by integrating them into the fabric of daily operations, companies can manage their learning more effectively.

Learning organizations also recognize that human activities have rhythms, paces, and affective tones that collectively are called 'moods'. Moods automatically predispose individuals or teams to certain kinds of actions and close them off to others. For example, a team may be in a mood of resolution and ambition, of defeat and resignation, or resentment and rebellion. People in panic cannot speculate and plan, and people in a mood of resignation cannot evoke ambition.

Learning organizations train their team leaders to shift the moods of their teams to those that are consistent with the actions to be performed. When this skill is mastered, it is possible to design moods which alleviate stress and anxiety and promote serenity and wonder–moods not only conducive to better health and well-being, but also essential for learning and creativity. A leader who has learned how to shift the mood of his or her team from fear and resignation to trust and ambition has taken an important step in building a learning organization.

SUMMARY

Tomorrow's leaders will be those who *know* that teams – linked and balanced, self-directed units of people – will invariably outperform a loose group of individuals who operate together by chance alone, particularly in environments where multi-skilling, job rotation, informed judgements and consensus decision making determine performance. *Teams* can be deployed, refocused and motivated for action quickly. When a team is committed to tangible results, it can readily leverage the combined role preferences and skills of its members to achieve outcomes (*and* processes) beyond the competence and reach of less unified collections of employees.

It takes a particular type of person to enable a team to perform *synthesistically*. As J. R. Katzenbach and D. K. Smith, two McKinsey consultants, wrote in their book *The Wisdom of Teams* (Harvard Business School Press, 1992), '. . . most models of the so-called "organization of the future" . . . "networked", "clustered", "non-hierarchical", "horizontal" (organizations) . . . are premised on teams surpassing individuals as the primary unit of performance. When managers seek faster, better ways to match resources with customer need or competitive challenge, the critical building block is – and will increasingly be – at the team, not the individual, level.'

I wholly echo these sentiments. But I would add that tomorrow's leaders will come from those able to link, balance – to synthesize, in other words – high and sustained performance from the range of leadership guidelines developed by Procter & Gamble during their tremendous transforma-

改

tion during the period 1985–1991. Their guidelines make clear a leader's challenge and its rationale, but like many so-called 'loose–tight' organizations leave room for the leader and his or her team to determine their own process goals, timing and resources.

The Procter & Gamble Leadership Model

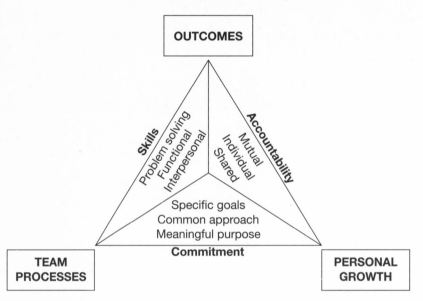

This model has been used as a tool by the Europe Japan Centre for transformational leadership education and development. It produces tomorrow's leaders from those willing to let go of conventional 'gung-ho' leadership styles and who understand the pivotal role of human dynamics in the process of pursuing and achieving corporate success.

4

HOW WILL TOMORROW'S BUSINESSES BE PLANNED?

改善

INTRODUCTION

In his book *The Ascendant Organisation** Peter Wickens wrote 'Leaders achieve results by working with and through people and exist at all levels in the organization.'

It follows from this, and from the idea that all employees can contribute to their company, can take ownership of their own development, can work in self-directed teams and be responsible for designing and managing work processes, that strategic and tactical plans should evolve from the meeting of a bottom-up fountain of ideas and a top-down cascade of broad corporate financial and trading objectives. If my contention that, in a Kaizen organization (or, an 'agile organization', a 'learning organization' or an 'aligned organization') leaders at the top should actively share the strategic vision and empower teams to structure their own work and working environment to achieve key performance indicators in a self-determined way, it is natural they should also maintain an open mindset and, as Wickens wrote, 'have the wisdom and judgement to employ good people and give them headroom'. I would add, 'and be receptive to contributions from anyone at a point of action'.

---

*MacMillan Press, 1995

改

In that the Information Age and its attendant technologies are making companies more transparent the planning process can no longer reasonably take place behind Chinese walls on the top floor. Like decision-making, it has to be pushed down to the lowest level of delegation. This is where companies find their 'critical mass', the bulk of their headcount and in which team leaders and other internal champions can exercise their influence to swing a workforce behind the corporate vision, goals and objectives, thus aligning the company throughout. In this environment, plans can be presented, discussed, brainstormed and redrafted vertically and laterally, thereby encouraging all-points ownership and eliminating the feeling that someone else's plan is being imposed.

Clearly, I am not saying that planning becomes a free-for-all, a fun exercise used purely as a device to stimulate participation in company and department affairs. In Kaizen organizations the planning process is a controlled process with expectations, deadlines and means explicitly spelled out; but cross-company and inter-team discussion and peer review is nonetheless demanded. Once again, my earlier point about managers/leaders letting go, trusting their people to contribute *positively* and monitoring from the boundaries has currency here: managers and leaders who have for generations seen planning as one of their functional specialisms must come to terms with the loss of this role-defining task. However, it is not total loss, simply a change in emphasis. See diagram opposite:

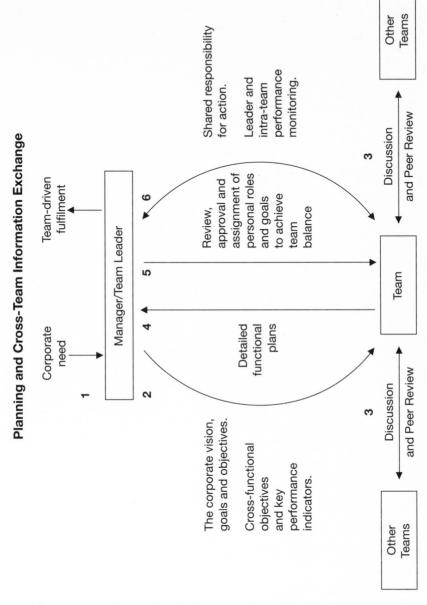

Planning and Cross-Team Information Exchange

This schematic illustrates Akio Morita's view that tactics should be left to subordinates while strategy should be the prerogative of the chief executive. In Sony, chairman Morita practiced this credo – first, spend your time correctly judging future trends; second, leave details of daily operations to the responsible personnel; third, insist that they make consensus decisions; and fourth, always approve what they ask to be done for short-term tasks.

THE KAIZEN APPROACH TO PLANNING

As you know Kaizen is predicated on continuous improvement, a non-ending and painstaking examination and questioning of current processes and standards. So it is in planning, which begins (if, indeed, there is a clear beginning) with a critical appraisal of current goals and objectives and their continuing validity and relevance to the long-term vision. That vision – and, hence, the corporate mission – may hold good for many years, but short-term goals and tactical objectives could well have been modified and improved during the course of a trading year. This willingness to adapt goals and objectives and to make plans flexible sets Kaizen organizations apart from others, in which strategies can become inflexible millstones that compromise performance and prevent adaptation with the speed that opportunities or threats might demand. To put it somewhat basically, some companies formulate an annual plan (which may or may not draw on lessons from the previous year's plan and performance) and, like armies of the past, move forward, line abreast, into the teeth of competition. Kaizen companies are more like today's rapid reaction force: swift, responsive and adapting to prevailing conditions as they change. In this sense, a leader's ability to communicate, command and control – to swing his or her team behind changed plans – is of paramount importance. Peter Wickens wrote,

> '*Aligning* the organization is of critical importance. In simple terms this means that all parts of the organization are working together to achieve the same objectives. But it does not happen by chance. First, the goals and objectives must be understood

and shared and secondly, each part (that is each team) must ensure that its activities complement those of others and do not work in opposition. This does not mean that everyone behaves in exactly the same way, but . . . in the ascendant organization there are no Chinese walls and it is the leader's task to ensure that none arise. In addition, the leader has continually to be challenging the organization to improve.' (Parentheses added.)

With a focus fixed firmly on improving every aspect of the way the organization goes to market, and an inherent flexibility borne of the understanding that a plan should last only until the objectives it serves and the internal and external conditions it reflects change – as inevitably they will – planning in Kaizen companies is a continuously rolling activity. Nevertheless, short-term tactics and goals always relate to the big vision and its long-term aims, and, until this changes, performance-improvement planning – in team meetings, Kaizen groups, cross-functional project groups and supplier/customer/principal meetings – is an integral part of every working day. In 'Leadership Excellence in the 1990s: Learning to Love Change'* Tom Peters wrote,

'The most efficient and effective route to bold change is the participation of everyone, every day, in incremental change.'

Transformational leadership is an important ingredient in Kaizen planning. Some employees can feel powerless, disenfranchized even, in an environment where planning is not the traditional annual event and plans are infinitely adaptable rather than being set in concrete for the next 12 months. It's

---

*Journal of Management Development, Volume 7, Number 5, 1988

之又

a case of changing their mindset, and this is another leadership task. In Kaizen companies in Japan *everything* is written down, noted and recorded, and a plan is in one sense nothing more than a record of *current* thinking. Dynamic thinking and opportunity-spotting will of course change current thoughts (and their consequent actions) thus generating a new record, a new plan. Expressed in this way, planning is thinking and plans are a way of capturing thoughts for everyone to see, share and discuss. The fluidity that can upset employees can thus be presented as revisions that constantly renew what has to be achieved. Paradoxically, the constant improvements provide constant stability, for in Kaizen it is the *same* plan, rather than a number of discontinuous plans, that evolves through different versions or generations. Ultimately, of course, a plan can be so transformed that it is markedly different from how it started, but better that it is reshaped by evolutionary changes than a revolutionary operational break. What I mean is shown in the simple illustration opposite.

A leader's task in this scenario is to present planning and changing plans as essentially a human-centred activity that is merely the dynamic response to the realities of the marketplace; in other words, transformations are the consequence of creative thinking and communicating, not the cause of change for its own sake. They derive from never being satisfied with today's standards, with the *status quo*, and strategies and plans are consequently simply management tools that must be constantly innovated, sharpened and refocused when the going gets tough.

Peter Wickens summed this up very well:

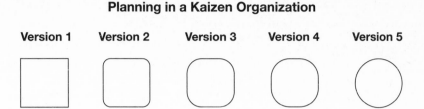

Planning in a Kaizen Organization

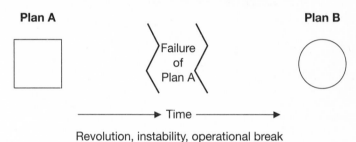

Evolution, stability, operational shift

Planning in a Traditional Organization

Revolution, instability, operational break

'. . . the leader does not actually have to have a precise vision from the beginning. The leader's responsibility is to provide the spark which defines the broad direction and creates the environment in which all the people in the organization can put flesh on to the bones, and often make fundamental contributions to the direction of the organization and the detail of needed changes.'

The guiding principle of planning in Kaizen companies is rigour, not rigidity.

In many ways the flexible and inclusive approach to planning in Kaizen companies reflects the milestone thinking of H. Igor Ansoff who, in his seminal and outstanding book *Corporate Strategy**, wrote,

---

*McGraw–Hill, 1965; Sidgwick and Jackson, 1986

改

'Objectives are a management tool with many potential uses . . . In the strategic problem, objectives are used as yardsticks for decisions or changes, deletions and additions to the firm's product – market posture.'

He observed that identifying a competitive advantage requires of company leaders 'uncommon skills in anticipating trends'. In his *Implanting Strategic Management** he stated what every Kaizen leader knows, that an organization's performance is optimized when its external strategy and internal capability and plans are all matched to the turbulence of the organization's external environment. Given, then, that markets are highly turbulent today it is no surprise that Kaizen companies invest so much in their human resource and technology and ensure that strategic plans never stay on anyone's desk long enough to gather even a speck of dust.

Kenichi Ohmae, former chief of McKinsey's Tokyo office, is one of only a few Japanese management theorists and practitioners of world-class standing. In one of Ohmae's best-known books, *The Mind of the Strategist*†, he captured the motive force behind planning in many Japanese businesses when he wrote:

'In what I call the mind of the strategist, insight and a consequent drive for achievement, often amounting to a sense of mission, fuel a thought process which is basically creative and intuitive rather than rational.'

He defines creative insight as,

'the ability to combine, synthesize or reshuffle previously unre-

---

*Prentice–Hall, 1984 and 1990
†McGraw–Hill, 1982

lated phenomena in such a way that you get more out of the emergent whole than you have put in.'

He goes on to make the case for continually questioning the relevancy of current plans:

'If, instead of accepting the first answer, one . . . persists in asking "Why?" four or five times in succession, one will certainly get to the guts of the issue . . .'

Ohmae is an iconoclast, renowned for shifting his ground, yet often he encapsulates a trend succinctly, a trend that sooner rather than later becomes a reality. In *The Borderless World**, for example, he wrote:

'Too few managers consciously try to set plans and build organizations as if they see all key customers equidistant from the corporate centre . . . The word "overseas" has no place in Honda's vocabulary because it sees itself as equidistant from all key customers.'

Here he is emphasizing the importance of globalization, but whereas Porter, for example, is a powerful advocate of the Western approach to planning – data collection, analysis, measurement, comparison, interpolation and rigorous objectivity – Ohmae reveals the Japanese penchant for taking into account the raw gut feel, intuition and unmediated perception of trained, knowledgeable and opportunistic people, whether they are leaders or subordinates. I applaud his willingness to include subjectivity in strategic planning and flexibility in tactical plans. It reflects the essential employee-centred nature of the Kaizen approach to planning, and that improvements are thought of and implemented by employees

*Harper and Collins, 1990

改

working in synergistic teams. Of course, leaders must not allow a 'finger in the wind' approach to dictate action, and Kaizen's cross-functional and consensual approach to decision-making ensures that 'pet theories' and cavalier thinking are filtered out. However, whereas only ten years ago conformity of thinking was the norm, many Japanese firms are now re-examining the style and impact of influential leaders such as Taiichi Ohno, Toyota's designer of Just-in-Time inventory control, Konosuke Matsushita and Soichiro Honda and positively encouraging maverick and entrepreneurial thinking. Naturally, this will influence strategists' minds: we may yet see in Japan businesses taking quantum strategic leaps with much greater frequency.

STRATEGIC CONTROLS

In his new book *The Superchiefs** Robert Heller wrote:

> 'Every company needs a plan which, as management professor Brian Houlden says in his book *Understanding Company Strategy*, describes what kinds of activity it will engage in, the resources needed, the main steps, the people responsible, the key signals or "milestones" and the external factors to be reviewed.'

But Michael Goold and John Quinn added in their book *Strategic Control: Milestones for Long-Term Performance*[†] that without strategic control strategic planning is fairly useless.

---

*Mercury Books, 1992
†The Economist Books Ltd/Hutchinson, 1990

Goold and Quinn make the point that strategic controls are not exclusively synonymous with financial controls:

> 'exclusive focus on financial results and budgets does not encourage managers to invest and build for longer-term competitive advantage'.

Houlden in *Understanding Company Strategy* stresses,

> 'Organizationally, growth businesses need greater freedom to grow vigorously . . . entrepreneurial enthusiasm should not be discouraged by over-zealous criticism.'

So what controls, other than growth in turnover, profit margins, return on capital employed, and level of borrowing, will achieve control aims without smothering initiative and entrepreneurship? Essentially, the controls should measure strategic progress. In Toshiba, for example, there is no direct link between either financial or non-financial targets and personal career promotion or bonuses. The thinking behind this is not to reward past performance when the present (at which time last year's figures are being finalized) might already be showing signs of deterioration; rather, as Heller says,

> 'how a profit is made may well be more important than how much.'

He suggests

> 'a profit earned through reducing costs by more than falling sales, for example, is plainly less worthwhile than gains which come from expanding sales more rapidly than costs.
> 'The first profit means either a declining market share or a declining market; the second implies a powerful surge in either market or marketing strength or both. Of course, taking out cost is a continuous test of good management. But again the "how" matters . . .'

and it is *this* against which strategic progress is measured and, subject to how it stacks up against key performance indicators, earns reward.

This clearly differentiates companies like Toshiba from such financial control companies as Hanson, whose managers work and respond to a very traditional Western system of targets and incentives to which are applied quite strict short-term investment payback criteria.

Again, we are seeing the importance of *process* in the Japanese system: the 'how' is as, if not more, important than the 'what', the results. 'How' implicitly encourages creative thinking.

This is the style of 'continuous renewal' thinking to which many Western managers have been averse for too long. The Kaizen system 'scores low on short-term pay-offs and high on current spending', as Heller puts it in *The Superchiefs*.

> 'Such managerial short-termism is enshrined in reward systems, with individual managers targeted and assessed on short-term performance, and in investment appraisal, through too high and too early target rates of return.'

He goes on to equate limited horizons with limited planning and limited delivery: a 'closed loop' in which sparkling short-term profit becomes the substitute for planned long-term growth and product development.

To return to Ansoff's book, he reduced the strategic success formula to sets of clear statements, starting with the observation that return on investment – a classic financial control – is the product of six inter-related functions. These are production efficiency, marketing effectiveness, socio-political sensitivity, market profitability, product attractiveness, and socio-political acceptability. As I remarked earlier, Ansoff's dictum that strategy must match environment, and capability must match strategy and both must match the degree of environmental turbulence, demands that strategic controls monitor and measure how well progress is maintained in only partly predictable markets, using novel and creative approaches.

To be precise, once a strategy has been handed down to its implementers it should be left to them to travel the journey and gain recognition from not only achieving the desired results but also for the processes employed. This approach, very much based on trust, recognizes that action, progress and strategic control rest on each leader's competence. Ansoff put it like this: During shifts in turbulence general management capability becomes critical to success. Heller asks, 'So what sort of capability do you need?' He suggests that 'strategic myopia' can easily overcome leadership. By this he means on the one hand, a leader can be so primed to achieve results that he or she disregards the processes and people needed to fulfil the raw financial outputs, and on the other a leader can work in the here and now only, forgetting the past. Heller says,

> 'Forecasts that are discontinuous from the past (using an entirely new Plan B when Plan A fails) trigger neglect, rejection and paralysis by analysis. At the lowest level of turbulence, you can get by with the custodian manager (leader) who likes to preserve the status quo, suppress risk and play internal politics – but as turbulence rises, so the need moves upwards to controller and growth leader, and then to entrepreneur and finally creator.' (Parentheses added.)

改

(see previous diagram on page 127)

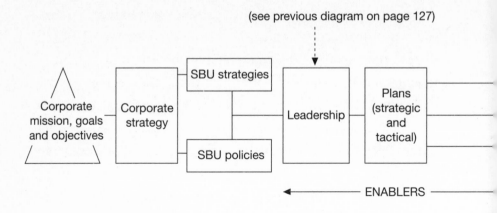

So, strategic controls need to be both qualitative (measuring the quality of the strategy 'enablers') and quantitative (measuring the quantity of the strategy 'outcomes'):

In the above diagram there are five 'enablers' and four outcomes':

1 *Leadership* is measured by how well the executive team, managers and team leaders communicate the corporate and SBU objectives and strategies, and inspire their people to generate a bottom-up fountain of contributory planning ideas.

2 *Plans* are measured by how completely SBU/functional teams incorporate the long-term view in their short-term goals, and how such factors as determination, communication, implementation, review and continuous improvement are also incorporated to ensure action is driven directly by the plan.

3 *Team management/Individual management* is measured by how well leaders release the full potential of their people, and how well this is used to transform the vision into reality.

Strategic controls: enablers and outcomes

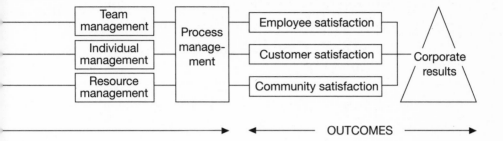

4 *Resource management* is measured by how appropriately (that is time-, cost-, and need-efficiently) leaders and their people identify and utilize plan-implementation finances, information, materials, technology and physical space.

5 *Process management* is measured by how well principal and support processes are designed, developed, utilized, reviewed and revised to fulfil the initial plan and any subsequent changes to it.

These five enablers are concerned exclusively with how the strategy is progressed. The following four outcomes are concerned with what leaders and their teams produce:

1 **Employee satisfaction** is measured by changes (since their previous assessment) in people's feelings, competencies, needs satisfaction and expectations.

2 **Customer satisfaction** is measured by customers' perceptions and purchase satisfaction.

3 **Community satisfaction** is measured by the impact on the company's civic community of its presence, protection of

the local environment and its preservation of both global and local natural resources.

4 **Corporate results** is measured by what the company is achieving relative to its planned performance, and how well the results satisfy the needs and expectations of financial stakeholders.

Naturally, all measurements are made against control standards, or key performance indicators, in each case.

HEWLETT-PACKARD

Director of Hewlett-Packard Laboratories in Bristol, UK, Dr John Taylor, explained to me how the company has developed around a number of deeply-held values and beliefs concerning H-P's people, business and management. These reflect so much of what I have been saying in this book, and they illustrate the strong framework that has kept the company aligned through the peaks and troughs of operating since Bill Hewlett and Dave Packard began trading from Bill's garage in 1939.

People

- most people really want to do a good job, so you should begin by trusting them

- good people aren't motivated primarily by money – they basically want the satisfaction of doing a good job

- if people are going to perform well, they need the right environment, the right tools and they need to have agreed objectives which reflect the mission of the company and which they understand and buy into

- people can only take ownership for doing their job well if they are trusted with the information they need to know how well they are doing it, and the authority to improve the processes involved in doing it

- reward people for their actual contribution to the job, rather than for their qualifications or future potential, no automatic pay rises

- tell me how you're going to measure me and I'll tell you how I'm going to behave.

Business

- the company should focus on how to add high value for its customers by understanding and meeting their real needs, so that its business generates sufficient profits to fund its growth; sustainable growth funded from good profit margins is more important than buying market share at any price

- 'stick to your knitting' – the company should grow around an evolving set of organic technical competencies through which it delivers real value to its customers, rather than being a trading conglomerate

- if you try and rip society off, sooner or later it will get its own back

- build a reputation for unrivalled quality, integrity and long-term commitment to meeting your customers' needs

- if somebody is going to make your products obsolete, it had better be YOU.

▶

Management

- 'management by wandering around' – informal, personal hands-on listening is a very effective way for managers to know the state of the organization and to detect and correct problems early

- a manager should always add value not just observe and transmit

- manage 'loose-tight' and lean and mean; don't stint on the fundamentals of environment and equipment, people and training, but don't waste a cent on frills and status symbols

- single status – give people what they need to do their job, open plan, open door, same pension plan, same restaurants, etc.

- people should develop the authority of competence, not rely on positional power and rank in the organization

- balance recognition of great teamwork and individual excellence of contribution – team celebrations and personal recognition by managers are as important as cash rewards.

(As I mentioned, Bill and Dave started Hewlett-Packard in Bill's garage. 50 years later, in 1989, the State of California designated the garage a California Historical Monument and 'the birthplace of Silicon Valley'. Bill and Dave attended the opening celebration, somewhat reluctantly, saying, 'We don't see what all the fuss is about. This old garage is ancient history and what we care about is the future of the company – the next 50 years. Now what do you think about the latest development in . . .'!)

SUMMARY

- In the words of Henry Mintzberg in *The Nature of Management Work**, business strategies are 'crafted'. Plans evolve as leaders and teams reconcile stability and change with turbulent markets, and think, act and review to achieve balance between the here and now and the future and between short-term and long-term goals.

- They emerge and are controlled most effectively under the guidance of those with a passion for their company, its people, its customers and the community at large. These are the leaders who inspire their people to plan, do, review in a continuous cycle of improvement, and can motivate uncertain employees to accept the very nature of dynamic planning as a tangible sign of creative thinking.

- In its turn, this leads to what has been called 'breakthrough' thinking, which is a sure sign that the company is a learning – or agile – organization.

- Controls should focus on how strategic progress is being achieved (or, conversely, how it is failing) as well as what strategic results are being produced.

- This means looking beneath the surface and measuring qualitative factors such as the enablers shown in the above diagram. The value of process understanding is critical to achieving the desired results.

---

*Harper and Row, 1973

5

HOW CAN WESTERN BUSINESSES GEAR-UP FOR OPEN LEADERSHIP?

改善

INTRODUCTION

Kaizen leadership is open, visible, accessible, communicative, sharing and empowering. It is process orientated; in short, Kaizen leaders train, motivate, inform and empower – they *enable* – their people. Kaizen leaders are *made*, not born; the only thing that birth and experience will have given them as preparation for the long and intensive training and development required to think and act like a Kaizen leader is an open mind. As Peter Wickens said in his book *The Ascendant Organisation*, 'the key to success is not a greenfield site but a greenfield mind!'

Kaizen companies, too, are made; the only things which a CEO needs to effect the shift from a traditional Western corporate culture are a willingness to consider blending-in Kaizen, understanding that Kaizen is not an *overnight* cure for corporate ills, phenomenal stamina and commitment, and an unswerving focus on the goal of creating a new style of company.

Given these fundamental ingredients any company, large or small and in any business sector, can become a Kaizen organization. However, Kaizen is not a bolt-on panacea or palliative; its introduction must be led from the top and implemented deep in the heart of the organization. There

改

will inevitably be difficult times and doubt that 'reculturing' the company is a good thing or can be achieved. Gaius Petronius wrote in the 1st Century AD,

> 'We trained hard and it seemed every time we were beginning to form into teams we would be reorganized. I was to learn later in my life that we tend to meet every new situation by reorganization. And a wonderful method it can be for creating the illusion of progress while producing confusion, inefficiency and demoralisation.'

It will take a great deal of personal and commercial courage to embark on a programme of internal change when external markets are so turbulent; but if a SWOT analysis clearly reveals a poor fit between Strengths and Opportunities and a dysfunctional correlation between Weaknesses and Threats, something must be done. And rather than doing just *anything* it is likely to be more effectively constructive to embrace a proven philosophical, values and practices system, such as Kaizen, bearing in mind that Kaizen-based systems are powerful influences for giants like Nissan, Toshiba, Komatsu, Matsushita, Unipart, Rolls Royce Engines, Boeing as well as smaller companies such as Braitrim, Bard UK, Paddy Hopkirk's company and a tiny hotel in Tokyo, Daiichi Hotel Annex, that shot to the top of the Nikkei Trendy Index (a regular survey of hotels which ranks big and small, chain and private hotels according to their facilities and quality of service).

What follows is less prescriptive than it is indicative, though it is based on my own experiences, and my colleagues' in London's Europe Japan Centre, with many companies which have decided that the best from the East and the West could provide the process, relationship and results improvements needed to prosper. But above all, most CEOs with whom I have discussed Kaizen and worked to introduce it have been looking for a single, structured, co-ordinated and coherent change programme that integrates quality, processes, customers, suppliers and employees in a synergistic whole. One might easily use the jargon 'holistic' when talking of Kaizen.

GEARING UP FOR CHANGE

I am sure you do not need reminding that, before and during the introduction of an initiative of the magnitude of a Kaizen change programme you (if you are the CEO) should *not*:

- own the initiative as 'your' initiative and impose it from the top
- suggest that it will quickly cure any performance problems
- rely on your personal vision, without converting it to a considered and detailed long-term action plan
- believe that by changing (that is, developing or improving) structures and processes only you will achieve your objectives
- believe you know all the answers – indeed, even all the questions
- start before you know clearly what it is you want to achieve
- believe you can throw out the old culture, values, processes before the new ones have been totally accepted by the workforce: the old and the new might have to co-exist

for some time. If the old is, in fact, so incapable of sustaining survival or supporting progress it suggests that insufficient investment has been made in it in the past, and if this is the case you need to ask yourself three questions:

1 Could the impact of a potentially 'alien' system of beliefs and practices like Kaizen's cause the old to finally collapse before the new has 'bedded-in', thus leaving the company exposed?

2 If investment in the past has been so sporadic or non-existent what evidence do you have that there will be sufficient now to introduce, nurture and develop the new?

3 Would it be wiser to first strengthen the old to bring it up to a better Western standard, and then blend-in Kaizen?

I developed a standard Europe Japan Centre model which I call 'The Route to Introducing Kaizen Values'. It illustrates, in a simple outline way, how to manage the transition from old to new. The schematic is shown below; following it I amplify the steps in a detailed explanation.

The Route to Introducing Kaizen Values

Before embarking on any phase it is essential that the aims of the change are clear: Why do you want to do this? What do you want to get out of it?

Phase   Steps

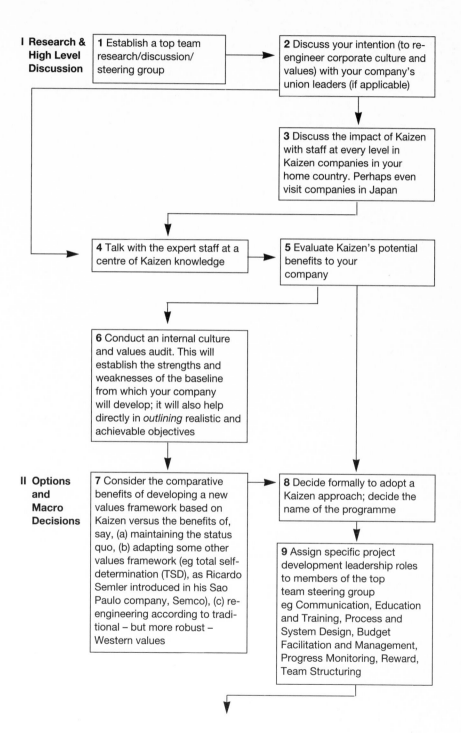

**I Research &
High Level
Discussion**

1 Establish a top team
research/discussion/
steering group

2 Discuss your intention (to re-
engineer corporate culture and
values) with your company's
union leaders (if applicable)

3 Discuss the impact of Kaizen
with staff at every level in
Kaizen companies in your
home country. Perhaps even
visit companies in Japan

4 Talk with the expert staff at a
centre of Kaizen knowledge

5 Evaluate Kaizen's potential
benefits to your
company

6 Conduct an internal culture
and values audit. This will
establish the strengths and
weaknesses of the baseline
from which your company
will develop; it will also help
directly in *outlining* realistic and
achievable objectives

**II Options
and
Macro
Decisions**

7 Consider the comparative
benefits of developing a new
values framework based on
Kaizen versus the benefits of,
say, (a) maintaining the status
quo, (b) adapting some other
values framework (eg total self-
determination (TSD), as Ricardo
Semler introduced in his Sao
Paulo company, Semco), (c) re-
engineering according to traditional – but more robust –
Western values

8 Decide formally to adopt a
Kaizen approach; decide the
name of the programme

9 Assign specific project
development leadership roles
to members of the top
team steering group
eg Communication, Education
and Training, Process and
System Design, Budget
Facilitation and Management,
Progress Monitoring, Reward,
Team Structuring

改

Phase   Steps

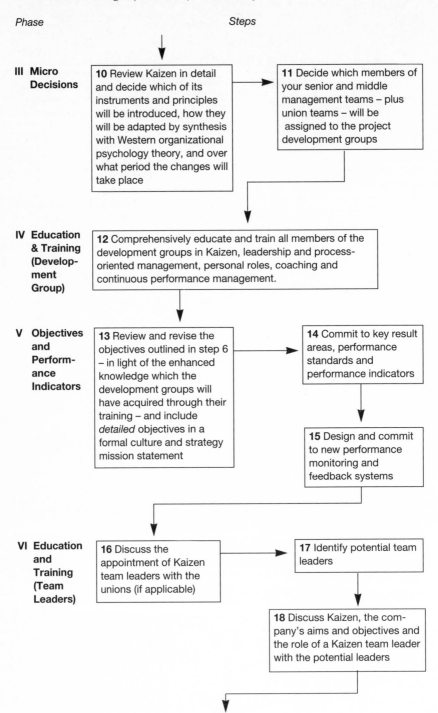

III **Micro Decisions**

10 Review Kaizen in detail and decide which of its instruments and principles will be introduced, how they will be adapted by synthesis with Western organizational psychology theory, and over what period the changes will take place

11 Decide which members of your senior and middle management teams – plus union teams – will be assigned to the project development groups

IV **Education & Training (Development Group)**

12 Comprehensively educate and train all members of the development groups in Kaizen, leadership and process-oriented management, personal roles, coaching and continuous performance management.

V **Objectives and Performance Indicators**

13 Review and revise the objectives outlined in step 6 – in light of the enhanced knowledge which the development groups will have acquired through their training – and include *detailed* objectives in a formal culture and strategy mission statement

14 Commit to key result areas, performance standards and performance indicators

15 Design and commit to new performance monitoring and feedback systems

VI **Education and Training (Team Leaders)**

16 Discuss the appointment of Kaizen team leaders with the unions (if applicable)

17 Identify potential team leaders

18 Discuss Kaizen, the company's aims and objectives and the role of a Kaizen team leader with the potential leaders

Phase   *Steps*

```
                          ┌──────────────────────────┐      ┌──────────────────────────┐
                          │ 19 Comprehensively       │──────▶ 20 Appoint into role the │
                          │ educate and train all    │      │ most suitable candidates │
                          │ potential leaders in      │      └──────────────────────────┘
                          │ Kaizen                   │                   │
                          └──────────────────────────┘                   │
                                                                          │
                          ┌──────────────────────────┐◀─────────────────┘
                          │ 21 Initiate a programme  │
                          │ of training in the       │
                          │ interpersonal and team   │
                          │ management skills        │
                          │ required of Kaizen team  │
                          │ leaders                  │
                          └──────────────────────────┘
```

VII Processes

┌──┐
│ **22** Design and prepare new internal processes based on Kaizen's │
│ chosen instruments and principles.   │
│ Reconstruct the workforce into Kaizen workteams   │
└──┘

VIII Internal Communication

┌──┐
│ **23** Initiate a company-wide awareness communication   │
│ programme, clearly explaining Kaizen and setting up the   │
│ company's new culture, values, style, processes, objectives – and │
│ the underlying reasons (ie customer focus)   │
└──┘

IX Education and Training (staff)

┌──┐
│ **24** Begin a programme of staff education, information and │
│ enablement. Note that it might be necessary to deconstruct old │
│ attitudes before constructing behaviours consistent with the new │
│ values and team-based organizational structures   │
└──┘

X Implementation

┌──┐
│ **25** Put in place the performance monitoring systems   │
└──┘

XI Launch

┌──┐
│ **26** Formally launch the Kaizen programme at a company-wide │
│ initiation event   │
└──┘

XII Monitoring

┌──┐
│ **27** Monitor, evaluate and respond to the company's progress │
│ towards becoming a recognized Kaizen company   │
└──┘

Amplified Explanation

Before discussing the steps in the schematic in more detail, I wish to emphasize a number of broad points:

1 **Know what you want to achieve.** You may not be able to articulate every aspect of your vision, but a statement as vague as, for example, 'We must improve direction/sales/quality/commitment/use of resources' is too insubstantial. It is also wholly results-based. You should express *how* you want the improvements to come about and, wherever possible, lay down key standards markers to help others understand the difference between existing conditions and performance and what you want in the future; for example, a statement such as 'Within 12 months 50 per cent of the workforce will be participating regularly in small group improvement activities' conveys results and process conditions, as well as indicating the direction in which behaviours will move.

2 **Understand what it is you are embarking on.** By this I mean, not only understanding Kaizen and the concepts of integration, organizational agility and organizational learning, but also understanding the time, costs and sheer effort and energy it will take to complete the transition.

3 **Determine a strategy.** This follows from the first broad point above; but remember that, inasmuch as Kaizen compels evolutionary change via incremental steps do not expect your strategy at this stage to be anything other than a foundation, subject to constant refinement.

4 **Involve all your people.** By involving everyone – taking them into your confidence, in other words – change can

start at the bottom, with the critical mass of your work-force, while you lead strategically from the top. Additionally, by opening your thinking to those who (a) will be most affected by the change and (b) will be responsible for working the new processes and behaviours you will implicitly provide opportunities for contribution, participation and 'ownership', and demonstrate the openness that characterizes Kaizen organizations. (By closing down and shutting employees off from 'the top' it would be perfectly understandable if the workforce simply followed your lead blindly, unthinkingly – if they had not 'rebelled' beforehand. Kaizen needs **informed** and cogniscant employees to succeed.)

In their book, *Transforming the Workplace** J. J. Nora, C. R. Rogers and J. Stramy quoted Irving Bluestone, then the UAW director of the Union's General Motors department, commenting on the change programme starting at GM's Cadillac Engine Plant at Livonia, USA:

> 'Truly successful endeavours in employee participation in decision making are not developed by management and simply handed down to the union and workforce. A successful improvement programme derives from mutually agreed upon understanding in which the union and management are co-equal in planning, designing and implementing the employee involvement process.'

Surround yourself in your top team with the right people. As Peter Wickens said in *The Ascendant Organisation*, the members who will steer the change programme 'must have high

---

*Princeton Research Press 1986

改

personal credibility and be trusted; must be innovators, achievers and effective communicators; (and) must represent all parts of the organization and retain full normal responsibilities.'

When looking at the diagram 'The Route to Introducing Kaizen Values' certain objectives are shown:

Phase I Steps 1–6

Kaizen *must* be led from the top, not just in the sense of project leadership but also behaviourally. The irreducible dependence on the managing director and members of the top team to be Kaizen role models is absolute for a successful change from conventional Western practices. This group of executives must, therefore, fully understand Kaizen and be prepared to sell its benefits to unions and staff, and steer its introduction down through their organization. Large-scale research – at home and, if possible, in Japan – is vital, as is discussion with a centre of Kaizen knowledge whose consultants can help tailor the transformation process to suit the current baseline (determined by a values audit) on the one hand, and the (at this stage) outline objectives on the other.

It goes without saying that, instituting a paradigm shift needs constant hands-on management: it is not, of course, like changing a railway timetable when, at a certain hour on a particular day a controller throws a switch and all traces of the old schedule are replaced by the new; a new culture will take time – often years – to fully replace the old, and during the transition both will be perceptible until the *ancien régime* has completely drained out of the system under the propelling influence of the new. This is especially true if the new culture/values framework is perceived to be inherently 'alien'. British Airways' culture change programme (now a decade old) is still being refined; Unipart's adoption of Kaizen has, in the same sense, only just begun.

Phase II Steps 7–9

Step 7 is optional; the point of taking it is to be able to reassure doubters and waiverers that, compared to alternative values frameworks Kaizen is justifiably the most appropriate and beneficial philosophy to pursue.

Having decided formally to adopt Kaizen, perhaps under a different name (Step 8), the members of the top team steering group can take on specific project development responsibilities. The seven development roles shown in Step 9 are only the prime roles – others might be necessary according to the company's current state and its goals. In any event, the project leaders can now invest their intellectual capital in small-scale research on the detail and minutiae of Kaizen in preparation for . . .

Phase III Steps 10–11

Of Kaizen's many instruments, only a few can be introduced at any one time. To introduce Kaizen wholesale will likely scare more than stimulate. The project leaders should concentrate their in-detail review on these and, at the same time, consider how to blend Western organizational and management theory into the Kaizen framework. Also, an overall time plan must be designed.

At this point the intention to adopt Kaizen can be made clearer to senior and middle managers by bringing them into the groundwork reviews, discussions and planning, and assigning individuals to the project development groups. Union leaders, too, if applicable, should be included fully at this step (Step 11) to ensure that first, they have no cause to feel that Kaizen is being imposed and second, they have equal opportunity to share the transition and thus own the final product on behalf of and with their members.

Phase IV Step 12

Sufficient groundwork will have been completed by this phase for the detailed education and training, which the development groups can now receive, to be developed into a set of personal competencies. However, as a major part of the foundation of understanding could have been *self*-developed up to this point (if a consultancy has not been involved throughout) it could be incomplete. If this is the case it will be a worthwhile decision to invest in a structured awareness and skills programme from Kaizen experts, at Step 12.

Phase V Steps 13–15

This phase is the watershed phase in the transition from old to new values: the steps up to this phase have been fundamental, these and those to come are creational. The broad 'directional' objectives outlined at Step 6 can now be reviewed and refined to produce firm and formalized 'achievement' objectives, summarized in a corporate mission and values statement.

At the same time, the key result areas, standards of performance and the performance indicators that will be the signposts (or mile markers) along the route to fulfilment of the achievement objectives can be established. Similarly, new performance monitoring systems can be designed.

Phase VI Steps 16–21

It will be remembered how vital team leaders are to the enablement of employees. They have a high-profile role in every Kaizen company. Their qualities as motivators, trainers, communicators, leaders, counsellors, psychologists, resource managers, chairmen, are much more important than their age or task skills and experience. For all these reasons choosing the right team leaders is crucial to the fulfilment of the achievement objectives. Hence the time and care implied by the six steps in this phase.

However, it might not be wholly necessary to follow these six steps precisely. For example, Steps 17–19 could be included in a combined briefing, training and assessment centre, from which suitable candidates can be selected and appointed (Step 20). These people can then go on to developmental training to prepare them specifically for their team responsibilities (Step 21).

Phase VII Step 22

Trained team leaders are now available to be included in the

改

design of the processes with which they must work. Their ideas concerning workforce reconstruction will underscore and support their feeling of personal responsibility for the emergent teams.

Phase VIII Step 23

At this point the Kaizen initiative can be rolled out to the entire workforce. Every channel of communication should be used: group briefings, videos, help desks, newsletters, all-point notice board bulletins and posters, explanatory booklets and, most definitely, 'management by walking around' (MBWA) by the managing director, members of the development groups, team leaders and union officers. Of greatest prominence in all communication must be the new corporate Kaizen mission and values.

Phase IX Step 24

Staff training can now begin. This must be conducted by the team leaders. However, it might still be necessary, despite the communication and help activities at Step 23, to deconstruct die-hard attitudes and behaviours before educating staff in the new beliefs and processes: these must not be contaminated by abandoned past practices.

Phase X Step 25

The new performance monitoring systems can now be put in place, just prior to . . .

Phase XI Step 26

Launching the Kaizen programme on a specific date.

Phase XII Step 27

Finally, progress must be monitored to ensure convergence of behaviours with the values' aims, and to allow reinforcement coaching and corrective action to be applied with point-like precision. It is worth reiterating that introducing a new culture and values framework will not be completed overnight, nor over one week, month or year. The transition must be nurtured and refined over many years. Kaizen is not something which can be put in place and left. It needs to be improved continuously and become a natural part of the organization's development.

I recognize how relatively easy and linearly sequential the steps in the schematic makes the transition from Western to Western-plus-Eastern appear to be; I also acknowledge that the process might not be as formulaic nor as fast in actuality as the schematic suggests. For example, there will inevitably be a great deal of overlap as different project development groups work on their assignments; some steps could take longer to complete than others, thus delaying the completion of a phase; and some steps *will* take longer than others due to their possible complexity (eg Step 22) or the sheer number of employees who, for example, must be informed (Step 23) or educated and trained (Step 24). Nevertheless, such problems can be overcome – a detailed Critical Path Analysis (or fishbone diagram) is a necessary planning tool that will help

改

managers anticipate and cope with the dynamics of culture change. The overriding determinators of success, though, are goal focus, a commitment to succeed, communication (that is, keeping the workforce informed), motivation (that is, ensuring the workforce wants to achieve the objectives as much as the top team does), momentum (that is, maintaining the pace and direction of change not only during what could be a period of many months but also afterwards to ensure *review and improvement* are continuous elements of the new culture), and training to ensure that when the Kaizen initiative 'goes live' it is launched into a receptive, educated and willing environment that nurtures and sustains growth of the new values.

The key is to introduce Kaizen in the Kaizen way, little by little: get one improvement accepted and cemented into the new values framework before introducing another. Build each improvement/change step on the one before.

PILOT PROGRAMMES

In *Competing Against Time** G. Stalk and T. M. Hout discuss the value of pilot programmes and breakthrough teams. They wrote,

> 'Pilots are a good way to energize those parts of the organization where good people are ready to go and where local trial and error experimentation is the right way to get solutions.'

---

*The Free Press, 1990

They stress how important it is to protect pilot programmes and their implementers both physically and, importantly, politically from 'senior people with turf issues . . . .'

Pilot programmes can demonstrate what an organization wants to achieve, particularly when an early success will help generate the 'ownership', commitment and momentum necessary for a full programme roll-out. Stalk and Hout go on to say,

> 'In this way, the change process is neither top-down nor bottom-up, but really driven from the middle and co-ordinated at the top by those who settled on the vision. The able middle managers are in the best position to do the cutting-edge learning that will reshape the company's practices.'

Stalk and Hout describe breakthrough teams as multi-functional and multi-skilled managerial teams who come together for a specific task and a finite time to achieve radical outcomes, like, as Stalk and Hout express it, 'collapsing time in half' or substantially challenging the company's paradigm and assumptions, even its mission.

The downside of breakthrough teams is that they become élitist, working in different ways from the company norm, doing special one-off tasks and becoming exclusive and isolationist. On the one hand, a specifically-tasked and enabled team can be the very spearhead that an organization needs to cut into the folds of a staid and bureaucratic infrastructure but on the other, it must not be allowed to become proprietorial nor assume that its skills or the knowledge it acquires invests it with long-term power. A breakthrough team must be consensual within itself and required to share its experiences widely. (Their lessons might be unpalatable, but if these are to be converted into new competencies the CEO must be prepared to act on the message. Failure to do so is like killing the messenger, and demoralizing the workforce. Eventually, inertia will settle back and the old issues will perpetuate themselves.)

One thing to remember about a pilot programme is that while it will naturally be the subject of detailed scrutiny by the top team they must stand back and let the team leaders and front liners simply get on with it in the type of open arena environment that will prevail when the full programme goes live. Too much inspection can cause constipation, as a director once said to me! Peter Wickens again:

> 'Some leaders may inspire, but unless they achieve the hearts and minds conversion of the front liners and have the capability to make the inspiration last, the benefits will be but short-lived.'

In other words, a pilot programme is not just to prove that an initiative will work but also to find out why it might fail on a large scale and what its process and personnel weaknesses are. Pilot implementers – the doers – must be allowed to make mistakes, but if senior management *polices* them in their work they could be too concerned to show good results to allow inherent flaws to show through.

MAINTENANCE

I have remarked many times already that a switch to Kaizen leadership will not be an overnight affair; nor will it be a one-shot affair. I remember an army captain saying to me once that his new subalterns did not understand what the 'new leadership' meant; they either imagined that barking out commands was still the required style or that excessive politeness was expected. Neither extreme is the case, but it would take most of the young leaders a great deal of continuous training plus experience of many different situations to learn and acquire the right degree of leadership *finesse*, and then constant reinforcement to maintain a hands-off style while retaining sufficient presence to command, control and communicate effectively.

In that managers and executives in business are analogous to the army's captains, majors and ranks above, and the subalterns are analogous to an organization's team leaders, the top team must:

- maintain its commitment over the long-term, and ensure everyone recognizes their goal-focus in their behaviour and expectations

- maintain the right supportive environment, in which the positive behaviour of others is rewarded, good decisions are acknowledged and improvement ideas are encouraged from everyone irrespective of where they work, what tasks they perform, how long they have been with the company and their position in the hierarchy

- regularly and frequently measure progress against the current plan, adjusting the plan accordingly – or, enhancing communication, training, motivation and empowerment to enable people to achieve the plan's performance criteria

- encourage initiative, creativity, dynamic thinking and self-determination to create a sentient workforce capable of

ZX

responding to changes in the marketplace quickly and
competently – agilely, in other words

- ensure that career progression is based as much on process
  competence as results ability

- achieve balance between the interests, needs and expectations of all internal and external stakeholders, and balance
  within teams to ensure personal preferences, roles and
  tasks result in job satisfaction, work enrichment and goal
  achievement

- continuously communicate the values and practices of the
  new paradigm

- ensure continuous internal alignment

- never stop learning, sharing the lessons and intuitive
  insights

- maintain strategic control by, according to C. A. Bartlett
  and S. Ghoshal's article in *Harvard Business Review**
  quoting amongst others Unilever's approach,

  1 Building 'common vision and values' through an entry-level
    'indoctrination' course;

  2 Developing contact and relationships by 'bringing managers
    from different countries and businesses together' for man-
    agement training;

  3 Spending as much on training as on R&D;

  4 Employing the 'most promising overseas managers on short-
    and long-term job assignments at corporate headquarters';

---

*July–August 1990

5 Transferring 'most of these high-potential individuals through a variety of different functional, product and geographical positions'.

(And, I would add, maintain strategic control by actively participating in a consensual approach to decision-making and requiring a collaborative approach to decision implementation.)

- be prepared to take tough decisions; be patient; be accessible; and, above all, believe in the absolute rightness of what they are doing.

Value-driven companies are neither exclusively top-down nor bottom-up, but both. The US consultancy firm Miller/Ginsburg conducted surveys of the efficacy of companies' values statements, which indicated that values – especially *new* values sets – will not become more than rhetoric unless 'six necessities' are *seen* to be lived:

1 The board is fully involved;

2 The chief executive is the committed architect and first-level supervisor of the values;

3 Definition of the values, their priorities and a common language exists from top to bottom;

4 Values find their way into each management process used to lead the company;

5 Management is not the judge of its own success;

6 Values are taken into account in how people are paid.

As Konosuke Matsushita himself believed, profit together with every other aspect of a company will be driven by the

改

right values. And unless every aspect of the company *is* involved, and people are enabled, management will have thrown to the wolves the most powerful driver of all.

In Japan today, the value of slow-burn career development is being questioned. The traditional age-based promotion system resulted in many salarymen moving up the hierarchy ladder to general manager level almost irrespective of their ability to do the job. Employees with comparatively low ability could reach quite senior positions, but because promotion was virtually automatic managerial ranks swelled resulting in many managers being in non-jobs. Whilst this could be afforded in good trading times Japan's recent – and longest and deepest – post-war recession has made companies realize they can no longer afford their overmanned middle tiers. These people are now the first to be encouraged to take advantage of early retirement programmes, and those following them up the hierarchy are now sometimes promoted on merit rather than length of service.

Over two or three generations many of the uniquely defining characteristics of the Japanese style of business will have changed forever, as indeed will many of ours, as the goal which the Japanese are changing towards – a *meritocracy* – comes towards it with the greater Westernization of Japanese organizations, and the goal which we are pursuing – *synarchy* (people sharing power, decisions, development and change with their rulers) – comes towards us under the propelling influence of Japanese Kaizen businesses in the West.

Until then, however, East and West remain differentiated, though neither is – nor can afford to be – complacent about their unique qualities:

	The Kaizen Approach	The Classic Western Approach
Leadership	Evolves decisions	Formulates decisions
	Leads by consensus	Leads by position
	Needs all the details	Motivated by the 'big picture'
	Must harmonize and balance with the team	Operates independently from the front
Motivation	Team-centred, in the first instance	Individual-centred, in the first instance
	Team-based working	Individual-initiative based
	Regular and frequent meetings to share information	Irregular meetings to monitor progress and performance and make decisions
	Loyalty to the company	Commitment to one's profession
	Respect for authority	Challenge authority
	Holistic caring of employees	Concern for each individual at work
	Strong sense of duty to colleagues	Duty is more towards self and family
	Willingness to accept lower benefits in difficult trading times	Seeks to preserve benefits Objectives-based
	Relationship-based	
Internal processes	Measure and reward process competence	Access and reward results ability
	Long-term planning	Short-term objectives
	Problem prophylaxis	Symptom resolution
	Monitor systematically	Judge intuitively
	Continuous improvement	Sporadic innovation Quantum leap revolution
	Small-step evolution	
Training	On-the-job	Off-the-job
	Continuous	Sporadic
	Self-determined	Directed
	Tailored	Prescriptive
	Necessary	A reward
	Maintained even in difficult times	The first to be axed in difficult times
	Skills-based	Knowledge-based

Communi-cation	Continuously shared for the good of the company	Occasionally shared for the benefit of selected individuals

	The Kaizen Approach	*The Classic Western Approach*
	Open and non-proprietorial	Closed
	Is seen as the source of greater understanding and efficiency	Is seen as the source of personal power
		Satisfies egos
	Serves teams	Reaffirms private agendas and personal styles
	Reiterates corporate values and practices	Is separate from all other processes
	Is integral to the process of empowerment	Much is kept private
	Much information is public	

Even if they do not call the process Kaizen or continuous improvement, as we have seen, many companies have drawn on aspects of the Kaizen philosophy to take their businesses into the future. ICI sums up several of the benefits.

ICI

Sir John Harvey-Jones is credited with many achievements in his five years as chairman of ICI, Britain's largest chemicals multinational, during which the company was transformed from a shaky regional player into a global industry leader.

His best-known skills are motivation and leadership. But his greatest contribution to ICI's dramatic revival between 1982 and his retirement was much more specific: the transformation of its top executive team from a collection of rival advocates on behalf of individual businesses and territories into a cohesive body of true directors of the group's best interests.

Until all profit and operating responsibility was delegated unambiguously to chief executive officers below ICI's 'Executive Team' (its eight executive directors), the team tended to be diverted from setting the group's direction into management tasks.

Above all, it resulted in the provision of greater resources for ICI's growth business, and those where it has particular strengths.

The executive team now classifies all ICI businesses into one of four categories: growth businesses; cash cows; problem businesses; and new businesses. The team was now able to ask, and deal with, such key questions as 'Are we developing enough new businesses?' and 'Are we getting to grips with our problems?'.

The impact of this change on ICI's global competitiveness had been reinforced by the company's post-1983 shift away from an organization structure dominated by geographic territories under which most issues were handled on a local basis, to one in which 'international businesses' now have responsibility for the development of ICI's major growth activities.

Working closely with the territorial companies within each division, the heads of these businesses are required to ensure that the business strengths are developed on a truly international basis.

Some friction between the international and territorial legs of any such matrix organization was inevitable, but at ICI this interplay was generally constructive.

Mindful of the constant warring and bureaucracy which has bedevilled many companies' rigid matrix organizations, ICI recognized that the particular working relationship (and, by implication, balance of power) which is struck between a given

▶

改

▶ international business and a given territory may be inappropriate for others.

They stress, however, that the importance in global competition of improved organizational effectiveness – especially in relation to the role of the corporate centre – cannot be underestimated.

SUMMARY

My final comments are these. First, I remember talking to a team leader in a Western company which had recently adopted Kaizen; he said how he used to be a 'supervisor', technically highly-proficient and respected for his production competence but untrained as a leader. His 'power' over his subordinates was derived from his positional authority. Now, he says, he is a trained leader and enjoys the privilege of working *with* his *team* who, he added, want him as their leader not just because he is technically skilled but also because of what he can share with his people as a man. But he recognizes, too, that because his team has been empowered and because 360° appraisals are now the norm, when his team no longer wants him he might have to move on.

Second, at one of my seminars a delegate approached me and asked for my own principles of leadership, rather than me relating others'. I said that I believe leadership is about:

- being a 'servant leader'; that is, willing to work for as well as lead a team
- caring about the human dimension and, simply, liking people
- courage, both physical and emotional
- encouraging individuals' innate ability to be innovative and creative
- encouraging people to develop and grow
- listening to your own soul, especially when it tells you what action to take when you have invited feedback on your own personal performance

- visioning; that is seeing beyond the next horizon and the next and the one after that, but always keeping your sights fixed firmly on the here and now and the *immediate* future

- communication and communicating in a language your people will understand

- taking your people with you.

This is leadership in tomorrow's businesses. I strongly believe that if companies are serious about competing in the future then the management team requires the courage to be committed to heroic goals – goals that might lie beyond existing resources and the existing corporate culture. The truth is, business leaders must develop in their companies' people the faith that they can deliver against the hardest of goals by focusing attention on creating an environment that allows – and encourages – staff to be innovative and fully involved in the business. Only then will management succeed in gaining the courage to commit themselves and their company to a new philosophy and global leadership.

There is no single, prescriptive style of leadership or organizational structure required to generate this sort of collegiate approach to performance improvement. Looking at the companies I have mentioned in this book and others with which the Europe Japan Centre and I have worked (or, at least, discussed Kaizen), it is patently obvious how diverse are the character traits of their leaders at every level. They do nonetheless commonly share the vision of their respective companies and believe that a synthesis of the best from the East and the best from the West does or will give them the cultural driver to achieve objectives beyond the reach of conventional Western people and company management styles.

In its turn, this gives individual leaders the confidence to look beyond their immediate horizon and establish the foundation for their business tomorrow.

INDEX

改

改

Also from Pitman Publishing

KAIZEN STRATEGIES FOR CUSTOMER CARE

Patricia Wellington

Throughout the world companies are realizing that their success depends largely on the satisfaction of their customers. Many conventional customer care programmes are failing to provide this satisfaction.

This is where Kaizen strategies can make a vital difference. This approach (adapted to suit Western national and business cultures) goes way beyond the cheery smile or even a genuine desire to please. It embeds a fundamental values and cultural change within an organization.

Guidelines are given on how to introduce Kaizen principles into your organization and make them work; the ultimate objective being to show how you can improve your organization's bottom line by enhancing internal and external relations.

ISBN   0 273 61472 X   Price £25.00

Available through all good bookshops

Prices are subject to change without notice

Europe Japan Centre Training Programmes

All Europe Japan Centre programmes are individually tailored. Tuition is in small groups and is highly participative. The list below provides an indication of our main areas of expertise.

Awareness Sessions

Kaizen and Creativity
What is Kaizen and how can it be combined with Western creativity to form an unbeatable approach

Leadership of Tomorrow
The new role of senior management in creating world-class companies

Research and Consultancy

Our unique research programme (R&I) assesses the current state of your organization and begins the vital process of involving staff more fully

One-to-one sessions with senior managers provide advice and support on cultural change or particular aspects

Our consultants can work alongside your teams to advise on organizational and human resources changes

Seminars and Workshops to Develop Skills and Put Theory into Action

Implementing Kaizen

How to introduce a culture of continuous improvement, building on the strengths of your organization

From Managers to Leaders

How to inspire and develop your people

The Kaizen Approach to Customer Care

Using Kaizen to enhance your service to customers

Developing Effective Team Leaders

How team leaders can get the most from their teams in terms of productivity, efficiency and creativity

Creating Teams that Work

How to put together the right people, set guidelines, organize meetings and create results

Inter-team Co-operation

How to break down barriers between departments and work more efficiently across the whole organization

The Kaizen Toolbox

Practical tools and statistical techniques, from brainstorming to PDCA and Pareto analysis, to measure performance and improvements

The Kaizen Approach to Problem Solving

How to identify real problems, analyze their root causes and find creative solutions

Personal Development and Kaizen

Workshops to build the personal skills needed to embed Kaizen in the behaviour of everyone in your organization

Seminars and workshops can be arranged for all levels, from directors and senior managers to team leaders and team members.

Europe Japan Centre Services also include research on the Japanese market and Japan Briefings.

For further information or an informal meeting contact Pat Wellington or Catherine Davis at:

The Europe Japan Centre,
Nash House, St. George Street, London W1R 9DE.
Tel: 0171–491 1791   Fax: 0171–491 4055